CYBERSECURITY ENFORCEMENT
AND
MONITORING SOLUTIONS

ENHANCED WIRELESS, MOBILE AND
CLOUD SECURITY DEPLOYMENT

RICHIE MILLER

Disclaimer

Every effort was made to produce this book as truthful as possible, but no warranty is implied. The author shall have neither liability nor responsibility to any person or entity concerning any loss or damages ascending from the information contained in this book. The information in the following pages are broadly considered to be truthful and accurate of facts, and such any negligence, use or misuse of the information in question by the reader will render any resulting actions solely under their purview.

Table of Contents

Introduction

IT Security jobs are on the rise! Small, medium or large size companies are always on the look out to get on board bright individuals to provide their services for Business as Usual (BAU) tasks or deploying new as well as on-going company projects. Most of these jobs requiring you to be on site but since 2020, companies are willing to negotiate with you if you want to work from home (WFH). Yet, to pass the Job interview, you must have experience. Still, if you think about it, all current IT security professionals at some point had no experience whatsoever. The question is; how did they get the job with no experience? Well, the answer is simpler then you think. All you have to do is convince the Hiring Manager that you are keen to learn and adopt new technologies and you have willingness to continuously research on the latest upcoming methods and techniques revolving around IT security. Here is where this book comes into the picture. Why? Well, if you want to become an IT Security professional, this book is for you! If you are studying for CompTIA Security+ or CISSP, this book will help you pass your exam. Passing security exams isn't easy. In fact, due to the raising security beaches around the World, both above mentioned exams are becoming more and more difficult to pass. Whether you want to become an Infrastructure Engineer, IT Security Analyst or any other Cybersecurity Professional, this book (as well as the other books in this series) will certainly help you get there! But, what knowledge are you going to gain from this book? Well, let me share with you briefly the agenda of this book, so you can decide if the following topics are interesting enough to invest your time in! First, you are going to discover what are the most important secure protocols and how to implement them. Next you will learn about host or Application Security Solutions, endpoint protection, boot integrity; along with database security concepts, application security concepts, hardening various systems, whether it's an operating system or registry. After that, we'll cover disk encryption; hardware root of trust, TPM chip and the concepts of sandboxing. Next, we'll cover how to Implement Secure Network Designs using load balancers, network segmentation, virtual private networks, DNS, network access control or NAC, out-of-band management, and port security. Moving on, you will learn about access control lists or ACLs, route security, quality of service with implications of IPv6, port spanning, port mirroring, and port taps. We'll also talk about monitoring services, file integrity monitors and how to install and configure wireless security. We'll also cover cryptographic protocols, authentication protocols, methods, and installation considerations. Next, you will discover how to implement Secure Mobile Solutions, connection methods and receivers, mobile device management, enforcement monitoring, and several deployment models. After that, you will discover how to apply Cybersecurity Solutions to the cloud, using cloud security controls, high availability, and the subcomponents, including storage, network and compute. We'll also talk about various solutions, such as cloud access security broker, or CASB, Secure Web Gateways, along with cloud native controls. Next you will discover how to implement identity and account management controls. After that, we are going to cover authentication management, passwords, trusted platform models and hardware security methods. Lastly, you will discover how to implement public key infrastructure, along with the types of certificates, certificate formats, and certificate concepts. If you are ready to get on this journey, let's first cover what are the most important secure networking protocols that you should be aware of!

Chapter 1 Secure Networking Protocols

In the next few chapters we are going to cover secure protocols, but before we get into the details of what we'll cover, let's talk about why is this important. Well, secure protocols ensure communication is safe from hackers and also from prying eyes. It's critical to securing a company's data, intellectual property and competitive advantage. Ultimately a company's footprint, their reputation, their brand, your ability to maintain a job, their investor confidence, customer confidence, all of these things wrap up into one. Secure protocols help strengthen that security posture and make all of this possible or at least help to make all of this possible. We're talking about the secure protocols, not the non-secure ones. There are a lot of protocols that are insecure. I'm going to talk about the secure versions of those protocols and why we should use them along with the use cases. As we go through the protocols, I want you to think about each of these in your own environment and say, what are the use cases? Where can I use these protocols and make sure that I'm securing the environment as much as possible? Security should always be at the forefront of our thought process and looking for ways to secure and look for secure alternatives to the way we're doing things currently.

Secure protocols, whenever given the option, we should always be looking to choose the highest security possible when establishing communication over an unsecure or an insecure medium, such as the internet. Such things as FTP, we want to look for FTP secure or HTTP web traffic. We should be looking for HTTPS or HTTP secure. Same thing with SSL and TLS, which is the underlying mechanism that a lot of this security or secure communication will take place. Secure POP or IMAP. Another way to think of that is web mail. Let's go ahead and dig in a little bit deeper here and talk about networking protocols. There are three main areas I want to make sure you're familiar with just you understand how things connect when they're talking to a network. We have IP or internet protocol, and that is connectionless. It's a connectionless protocol that's responsible for network addressing, and it provides routing of packets between networks. It allows us to give a more human-readable name or an address to a specific host or a specific resource on the internet or on our internal network that allows us to route and send traffic. It's just like a house number on the block in a neighborhood. Each of those pieces make up the address of that specific house just like an IP address. Some of the IP address will denote the network. Some of it will denote the host within that network or that subnetwork. Next we have TCP. When you put those together, we have TCP/IP. Transmission control protocol, that is a connection, or anti-protocol, and that establishes connections between endpoints and also provides guaranteed delivery of packets. What happens, it sends out a packet, and there's a wait time or a time to live on that specific packet. If the host that it's sending to or communicates with doesn't respond back and acknowledge and say, I have that packet, I've received it within a certain period of time, then that packet is assumed to be lost, and the host will resend again. That's why it's guaranteeing that delivery. Then we also have UDP or user datagram protocol, and that's a connectionless protocol. It's quick, but there's no guarantee of delivery or its best effort. These three things together make up the basis of how we communicate over an IP network or over the internet. Perhaps a bit of a refresher to you, but in case you're not familiar with this, let's just cover very briefly the three-way handshake that takes place during a TCP communication between two hosts. A three-way handshake establishes that connection between two hosts. A client node sends a SYN packet, a SYN data packet, over an IP network to a server to determine if the server is open for a new connection. It's saying, are you available to talk? The target server must have open ports that can accept and initiate new connections. If in fact that's true, the server responds and returns a confirmation receipt, a SYN acknowledgement packet, a SYN/ACK. From there, the client node receives that SYN / ACK of the SYN acknowledgement back from the server, and it will respond with its own acknowledgement packet. It goes through that handshake process very quickly and establishes that communication. Now we know the basics at a high level of how that communication is initiated, let's talk about the secure protocols and the secure versions of some protocols you're probably already familiar with.

DNS SEC

First up is DNS Secure. DNS is the Domain Name System, and we're familiar with DNS is how we resolve web addresses to IP addresses. It allows us to browse the internet, type in a website, www.Google.com, DNS will resolve that through a series of servers that are out on the Internet, all the way down to the company servers, the company DNS servers within Google's domain, respond back with the host that is specific for the resource we're looking for, and then turn around and deliver that web page to the client. All of that happens very, very quickly. There is a secure version of DNS, and that is DNS Security Extension, or DNSSEC, that was designed to add security to the original DNS specification. DNS was not originally designed with security mechanisms in place. Remember, DNS was designed way back in the late 60's, and it was designed to make browsing or communication over a very large network very fast and very efficient. It's a hierarchical naming standard. Security was not a big thing back then. There may have been four or five hosts when things initially took off, so we don't necessarily know if the original designers envisioned, 4 billion, 5 billion hosts like we have today, but as things started to scale, it quickly became apparent we needed a way to secure some of this traffic. It was meant to be a massively scalable, hierarchical naming system that resolves URLs to IP addresses. All responses from a DNSSEC server, which is protected zones, are digitally signed and authenticating their origin. It doesn't provide confidentiality of the data, so it's not encrypted itself, but it does verify that the server is in fact a legitimate DNS server. It prevents such things as session hijacking and DNS cache poisoning, so a rogue DNS server can't be set up on the network and directing them to illegitimate resources. If we look at a DNSSEC example, let's say, for instance, we have a user, which is referred to as a resolver in DNS lingo, that resolver wants to connect to a web resource. Let's say for the example here we want to connect to www.Google.com, we want to browse Google's resources out on the Internet. The user would connect, type in Google.com into their web browser, it's going to contact the ISP's DNS server.

Everyone that connects to the Internet has a DNS server configured, typically from their ISP. So from there the ISP would then refer that up to the root of the Internet, which is dot, the root servers out on the Internet. In a DNSSEC example, there are signed certificates that go through the chain of resolution. As we go through all these different DNS servers, every DNS server above has a signed certificate for the DNS server below. We can follow that chain of trust to make sure that nothing was intercepted or manipulated in that path. ISP contacts the root, the root says, hey, I don't know exactly where that is, but I do know the servers that are authoritative for the.com domain so I'll go check there. It responds back to ISP and it then goes out and contacts the.com or the top-level domain, asks the same question. There's a sign-in key and a digital signature of google.com, the DNS server a level below. So from there, same process, it goes back to the ISP, the ISP then goes out and contacts google.com, which is the second-level domain. It has the DNS key, and it's able to resolve that, and what's happening here is that we have this chain of trust so that everything goes back up to the root so it can be verified all the way through the chain and we know that no one has manipulated anywhere in that process, two main security issues, DNS hijacking and DNS cache poisoning. We know for a fact that everything is secure, there's a chain of trust, and nothing's been broken or compromised in that path. We can rest assured that that DNS server's response is legitimate. We can verify the authenticity of that response and know that we're connecting to a legitimate resource.

SSH

Some other secure protocols I want to talk about is SSH, or Secure Shell. Secure Shell is used for logging into remote hosts. That can be routers, switches, or servers, and it operates over TCP. Remember, we talked about TCP versus UDP. TCP is going to be a connection-oriented protocol. It's going to connect over TCP port 22. An IP address is one thing? We connect to an IP address, but there are also ports. We can put :22 at the end of that, and it would tell the host that we're connecting to we want to connect over port 22. A server, as an example, could wear a lot of different hats. It could be a DNS server. It could be an Active Directory server. It could be a video server, a mail server, you name it. All of those different services operate over different ports. By specifying what port we want to connect to, we're telling that server what service we want to communicate with. When we're talking about different use cases, Secure Shell allows us to remotely and securely log into our routers, our switches, and servers. We can open up a command prompt on a remote server and type commands just as if we're sitting at that server, but we can do that remotely. It saves us the time and energy and effort of having to go to each individual resource, sit down, either a console cable or just connect directly in person to that resource; we can do it remotely. It makes administration much, much easier.

S/MIME

Next, we have Secure MIME, or S/MIME. MIME is the Secure/Multipurpose Internet Mail Extensions. It's a public key encryption and signing of MIME data. We're sending emails, we're securing email delivery. There are some challenges; however, I want you to be aware of the protocol, but there are some actual challenges in implementation. When we're doing this, we want to send and receive, encrypted email between two hosts, a sender and receiver. Well, both parties have to have a public key/private key pair for them to communicate. That's either issued from an in-house certificate authority or from a public certificate authority. From a corporate standpoint though, that end-to-end encryption can defeat malware scanners. In practice, a company may not want to have that in place because then they can't go in and inspect the contents of that email, and they can't scan for malware because that data is encrypted. There are ways to put different types of SSL decryptors along the perimeter, and in some cases, it can strip that information off and decrypt it at the perimeter and then send it on to the recipient, but it's problematic at best, so something just to be aware of.

Secure Real-Time Transport Protocol (SRTP)

Next, we have Secure Real-time Transport Protocol, or SRTP. It's a secure version of RTP. SRTP is a security profile for RTP, or the Real-time Transport Protocol, and it adds confidentiality, message authentication, and also replay protection to that protocol. And as you may guess, is used to secure VoIP, or Voice over IP, traffic. It's great in that it has minimal effect on the actual IP quality, of that Voice over IP service. We can add security without decaying or degrading the end user experience, and that's key here. We want to make sure that when someone picks up the phone that communication doesn't sound jittery or broken up, so there's no reason to not have Secure RTP in place.

Lightweight Directory Access Protocol over SSL (LDAPS)

Next, we have LDAPS, or Lightweight Directory Access Protocol over SSL. LDAP, as we know, is the Active Directory mechanism we use to log into Active Directory services and find resources in a Windows network, and that operates over both TCP and UDP over port 636. What that does is secures traffic between the client and server over SSL and TLS, Secure Sockets Layer and Transport Layer Security. It does require all DCs to have an X.509 certificate installed. It may or may not be completely viable in your environment, or you may have a very distributed environment where you don't have everything sitting on one server. You may have a root certificate server and then issuing service below, so it just depends upon how your individual infrastructure is set up. But for purposes of our discussion, just understand what LDAP Secure is. It's a way of securing Lightweight Directory Access Protocol, or LDAP, and the ports that it goes over, 636, TCP, and UDP. Also, understand the transport mechanism and how it secures that traffic using SSL and TLS.

FTPS and SFTP

Next, we have FTPS, or FTP Secure, File Transport Protocol over SSL. And what this does, as you can imagine, is secure file transfers that use SSL for encryption, or that Secure Sockets Layer. Encryption can be turned off if other encryption is in use. So, for instance, if we have IPSec in place, we don't need to double dip here. We can turn SSL off and still have a secure communication, or secure transferring of files. And that's going to operate over TCP ports 989 and 990. Getting back to use cases, FTP is a very popular protocol people use to upload and download files all day long. If we're inside of a network or we're connecting from the outside, FTP typically, those credentials are sent in clear text, we don't want that. We want to use something that's secure. We're going to make sure we use FTPS, or SFTP. They achieve the same end goal. But in the back of your mind, we should always be looking for ways to add security to the way we do things. If we need to FTP, let's look for FTPS or SFTP. SFTP or Secure FTP, that sounds just like we just talked about. And the net result is the same, but it's a different way of doing it. It's SSH File Transfer Protocol. Before, we were doing FTP over SSL. We're using SSH. It provides for remote file transfer, access, and also management. It gives us a little more functionality, and what it does is utilize FTP over SSH. The FTP is tunneled through that SSH connection. TCP transport protocol, Transmission Control Protocol, connection oriented. We're going over TCP port 22.

SNMP v3
Next, we have SNMP version 3. Simple Network Management Protocol has been around for a while. There's versions 1 and 2, did not have security baked in. And since we're talking about secure protocols, we're looking for version 3. SNMPv3 allows for remote management and reporting of IP devices. All the different IP devices within our network, we can turn on SNMP, set up our community strings, and go out and have a management server, and then all of our clients, or the things we're communicating with, we can set up alerts. We can configure some devices. We can

report on others to see if that device is up or down. If there's an alert, it can send a trap to that management server and allow us to report very quickly on the state of our environment, or the health of these different devices. Communication protocols can be intercepted and manipulated, it can potentially lend itself to a breach or release some type of denial of service or some other type of, degradation to our service. SNMPv3 will encrypt that data. Earlier versions didn't provide encryption, Wherever possible, if we can use SNMPv3, encrypt our data, encrypt our communication, we just take one more thing off the table that hackers were able to use or try to leverage to breach or otherwise to create performance for the end user. SNMP, whether it's version 1, 2, or 3, is going to utilize UDP port 161 by default.

SSL/TLS

Next, we have SSL and TLS. SSL and TLS is Secure Sockets Layer/Transport Layer Security. And just you're aware, SSL is the older implementation. TLS is newer based on SSL. What it does is adds confidentiality and data integrity by encapsulating other protocols. It's not a method of communicating in and of itself, but it's a way for us to add security to other protocols? We can encapsulate that data, and we can add confidentiality and data integrity by encapsulating other protocols. Confidentiality and data integrity are two prongs of the CIA triad, confidentiality, integrity, and availability. It initiates that stateful session with a handshake. As an aside in your environment, make sure all servers are patched for the Heartbleed Bug. That was an SSL/TLS vulnerability that hackers were using and leveraging out in the wild, Very important that all your servers are patched to avoid that vulnerability.

HTTPS

Next, we have HTTPS. HTTP is web traffic, so authentication of the visited website, as well as privacy and integrity of that data exchange. It allows us to connect securely to a web address or to a web resource, a web server, communicate with that web server, and that communication is encrypted. So our ISP doesn't see what we're doing. Hackers or someone else that's sniffing that traffic, they don't see what we're doing. It also provides that integrity and the authentication. We know that the person or the website that we're connecting with is in fact the website that we are looking to connect with. It's not a fake or a forgery. By the same token, the client could also authenticate to the server, although typically we're just worried about connecting or authenticating and verifying the integrity of the server that we're communicating with. It also protects against eavesdropping and man-in-the-middle attacks. If you see MITM, that abbreviation is for man in the middle, which means someone is injecting themselves into that communication. Remember the old example of Bob and Alice. The hacker injects themselves into that process. Bob thinks he's talking to Alice, but he's talking to the hacker. The hacker then relays that information to Alice, but he's manipulating that data along the way. Man-in-the-middle attacks can be remediated or protected against using encryption. Also bi-directional encryption of the communication between the client and server; we're encrypting communication, both ways, between the server to the client and also to the client to the server. Also just you're aware, it's TCP, TCP communication protocol over port 443.

Secure POP/IMAP

Next, we have secure POP and IMAP, so accessing webmail. When we talk about POP, or Post Office Protocol, or IMAP, we're talking about accessing webmail. We're doing that securely, again, using SSL and TLS. It's a way of encapsulating that data. Post Office Protocol, or POP, POP3 is the latest version. That's going to be TCP port 110 for normal traffic or 995 for SSL. Internet Message Access Protocol, or IMAP, that's going to be IMAP4 being the latest version, and that is TCP port 143 or 993 over SSL. We're talking about different ways we can secure our networks. If we require and mandate that we always use secure versions of POP and IMAP, we can cut down on eavesdropping. Mail, webmail specifically, is a big target for hackers because if they're able to access someone's email and scour through that, they can get a lot of information about who their friends are, the way they communicate, the words the verbiage, the language that they use. Then they can craft emails to other people and make it seem very convincing that it's coming from that person because they've gone through a bunch of emails. They know what they're interested in. They know what sites they visit, what resources, what they just bought. All of these things can put up a profile on a target or a victim, and then as that attacker crafts an email that's specifically geared towards that target, it seems very convincing. It's much more likely that that person will click on a link that's in that email or do some type of action or take some action on that email. And then as soon as they do that, boom, malware is installed on that system. It can go out and started downloading other pieces of software. It could potentially become a zombie in a larger botnet, or it could communicate back to some command-and-control server, allow a hacker to come in, gain a foothold on that system, start browsing through our network, find a way to jump over a pivot, jump over to another network, start accessing resources. As soon as they start to gain relevant privileges, install a back door and gained persistence, and then off to the races at that point. Let's see how much information we can possibly exfiltrate or steal from this network. Depending upon the type of hacker that they are, they may be very slow and steady, very stealthy, very surreptitious in their exploration of data, and they sit there for weeks or months or years where they could very quickly want to get in and get out or try to destroy data, and try to take the company down. It could be a very quick process, or it could be very long, and by the time we realize it, they're already in our backups and everything else. If we've got to restore, it's too late. All of these different things, securing our FTP traffic, securing our web traffic, Voice over IP traffic, and so on, all of these different things, as we secure them, we're doing what? We're building up a defense in depth. A layered defense. The more locks on the door, the longer it's going to take a hacker or someone who's trying to do harm to the company, it's going to take them longer and longer and longer to unlock all of those locks before they can get in. That gives us the opportunity to identify and notice that the breach is occurring or make it Difficult that we may not even notice, but it becomes such a laborious process that they just give up and go somewhere else where they may have an easier target.

Use Cases

We talk about different use cases. I don't want to dig in depth into each one of these and go off on tangents, but I just want to quickly bring these to your attention and have you think in the back of your mind, where can I tighten up security? Where can I add security or secure protocols in each of these different instances? More importantly than the individual protocol, understand why would you want to secure that type of traffic. Voice and video; we talk about time synchronization. Every computer or every host on that network needs to synchronize their time. It's important for directory services, for other applications that everything is in sync. Typically, in large environment, all of those devices will sync to an internal time synchronization server. Smaller environments are where individual users may go out and sync to a time server out on the internet? One of the military servers, that may or may not be the case, depending upon your specific environment, but it's important that those things are secure because, again, every piece of communication can potentially be hijacked, some type of man-in-the-middle attack or some type of data manipulation to corrupt data, denial-of-service attacks where you simply get in and try to infiltrate the network itself. All of these things should be triggering thoughts in the back of your mind, how can I secure these types of traffic? Email and web browsing. We talked about HTTPS. We talked about IMAP and POP secure and File Transfer Protocol. We talked about FTPS and also SFTP. If a hacker is able to sniff the network and monitor that traffic and they can browse our FTP servers or upload and download our content, they can, again, build a very detailed profile of what's important, perhaps steal intellectual property or things they're not supposed to have access to. But aside from the obvious, stealing data, they can build a profile and get very, very good very, very quickly of what's inside of our network, the applications, the services, the users, maybe the locations even. All of these things can be potentially gleaned from the files that they're able to download or even upload, viruses, malware. That defense-in-depth mindset will go a long way to securing the environment. The same thing with directory services - every time you log into a network, every time we browse for a specific resource, all of that communication is potentially going over unencrypted. We want to make sure we encrypt whenever possible. Remote access - we talked about Secure Shell. That should be a standard. It should be a given. There should not be a way to access hosts in an insecure fashion. Telnet, as an example. Get rid of it. Turn it off. Make sure it's disabled everywhere. Use SSH so that communication is then encrypted, whether you're protecting to router, switches, servers. Same thing with domain name resolution - DNS traffic over port 53. DNS traffic is a favorite for hackers to exfiltrate traffic because everybody has it. Everybody has DNS traffic internal. You also need to then go out to an external DNS server when you want to browse web resources. So firewalls will always have those ports open, and traffic can go very easily in and out of the network, or over port 53. Monitor for that. Monitor for excessive amounts. Baselining. Make sure that we understand what's normal. What are the normal packet sizes, what's normal data flow? That way, when there are very large spikes, it should be raising red flags. Wherever appropriate, secure zone transfers, making sure we don't have rogue DNS servers on our network. Security should be in place from the get-go. Talked about routing and switching, we talked about Secure Shell and ways to securely access all of these different devices within our network. But think about the additional ways you can secure routing and switching. We talked about port security, making sure we don't have rogue access points and rogue switches, Wi-Fi access points on the network. All of these things should be configured to check in or authenticate on the network. Then also, devices on our network that can scan for rogue access points to make sure that no one is just plugging into our network and trying to set up some evil twin or some rogue access point to either give out fake DNS information, fake DHCP information, man-in-the-middle attacks and more. Network address allocation, DHCP, same thing. We want to be monitoring to make sure that people are not trying to instantiate fake or malicious DHCP servers on our network. If we have DHCP security set up properly, those servers will check in, and if they realize there's already a DHCP server on that subnet, they'll shut down and not serve us requests. Then lastly, subscription services - that can mean a lot of different things depending upon what company and what industry you're in. Just think of all the things we've talked about so far and how you can secure whether it's a website, a service, or an application, how you can secure those individual piece parts. In summary we covered two main areas. We covered protocols and use cases. For protocols, we covered such things as DNS Secure, or DNSSEC, SSH, and S/MIME. We talked about SRTP, LDAPS, and FTPS, and also SNMPv3, SSL, and TLS. Also, HTTPS and secure POP and IMAP. These are all things that you're probably familiar with in their insecure versions, and we talked about the secure versions of these protocols to help strengthen that security posture and make the overall security footprint of your company stronger. Some use cases we talked about where voice and video, time synchronization, things like email and web and file transfer, along with directory services and remote access. Also, domain name resolution, routing and switching, network address allocation, and also, subscription services. Things that is useful and used every day within your organization, the ways you can avoid some common pitfalls, and also, again, strengthen those specific areas within your organization.

Chapter 2 Host or Application Security Solutions

In this chapter we'll be talking about Host or Application Security Solutions. We'll be talking about endpoint protection. We'll talk about boot integrity; along with database security concepts; application security concepts; hardening of various systems, whether it's operating system, registry; we'll talk about disk encryption; hardware root of trust and also the TPM chip; and then wrap up with the concepts around sandboxing.

Antivirus
When it comes to antivirus, they can detect viruses, malware, in some cases ransomware or crypto-malware, root kits. Well, AV software can be standalone. It can also be agent based or network based, and it can also be cloud based. In this specific instance, we're talking about host-based antivirus, which means it's going to run as an agent, typically, on that server or that PC or laptop. It can scan data on access, and it can also periodically scan the entire file system, much like their network counterparts or cloud-based counterparts. They can do things when you click on a file, when you go to save a file, or you can have it run every so often, maybe once a day or once every hour, and it will scan the entire system. Then if it finds something,

whether it's a piece of malware, a virus, it will either quarantine that specific piece of code and then send some type of an alert, an email, or it can send it off to a NOC or a SOC, a security operations center, and it can also report back the details of that specific piece of code back to the company's headquarters, whether it's Microsoft or Trend Micro or McAfee. It can send that information back so that it can be aggregated and correlated across all customers in the environment to see if that specific type of outbreak, whether it's malware, viruses, worms, if that's being seen in the wild.

Endpoint Detection and Response (EDR)
When it comes to securing systems on our network and within our environment, it's important that we have endpoint protection in some form or fashion, so applications and tool sets known as endpoint detection and response systems, or EDR systems, or sometimes they may even have threat detection in there as well. You might see endpoint detection and also threat detection and response, so it could be ETDR as well. Well, these things have a number of key features. Endpoint detection response key features are they monitor and collect activity on endpoints. It's not just an AV program, or an antivirus program. They can do additional things like monitor and collect activity, understanding when things are launched, how they're launched. They

can then analyze that data to identify threats, patterns, or indicators of compromise, or IoCs, and then automatically respond to identify threats, to remove or mitigate them, and notify appropriate teams, security personnel. And then lastly, forensics and analysis tools to research threats and also search for suspicious activities. An endpoint detection program, or an EDR, may be a standalone application, or could plug into a larger system, like a SOAR system, S-O-A-R. We've talked about SOAR systems before, but just to reiterate, we have a SOAR platform that can do a number of things. It can gather information from event logs. It can gather things from our security incident and event management or monitoring tools, our SIEM systems, and then also EDR systems, endpoint detection response. All of those things can feed into a SOAR platform, which in turn can then do some automation for us, whether it be ticketing, IT ticketing, change control. It can open up tickets to remediate certain things that it finds. And then also controls, like alerting or whitelisting and blacklisting. If we whitelist an application, it means allow only this application, or only the ones we have whitelisted. Or if we blacklist an application, it means allow everything except for the ones that are on the blacklist. Whitelisting would be deny everything except what's on the list, and then blacklisting would be allow everything except for what's on the blacklist? Alerting, whitelisting, and then also third-party tools. That SOAR platform allows us to integrate a number of different things, including EDR systems and automate to a much greater degree.

Data Loss Prevention (DLP)

DLP, or data loss prevention, detects potential breaches and exfiltration of data. Especially in the age of PCI we want to make sure that we are capturing any attempts to exfiltrate data from our network. It does endpoint detection, things that are in use, network traffic, things are in transit, data in transit, and then also data storage, or data at rest. It allows us to understand, is someone storing credit card information? It might scan the network and look for things that have a series of nine digits separated by dashes. That might be a Social Security number. Or it may have 16 digits or whatever numbers represent a credit card. Things that might be personally identifiable information and things that are a no-no to store from a PCI standpoint, it will search for that and make sure that we're not storing data that we're not supposed to be storing in insecure locations. Then also, when things are attempted to be exfiltrated or stolen or removed from our network, it will capture those things as well. Additional methods we can use these DLP technologies to identify if someone's trying to remove data from our environment, we can do USB blocking, we can do cloud based, and we can do email, we can check all of these things as well. Is someone inserting a USB drive into a computer and trying to pull data off the network? Are they doing it from a cloud instance? Are they trying to upload things to some type of cloud storage or cloud application? And then, of course, email, self-explanatory, is someone trying to email something that they should not be emailing? The types of data to secure, we have data in transit, data that's being sent over a network, whether it's wired or wireless. A VPN connection will encrypt the data while in transit, wired or wireless. That could be a good thing or a bad thing. It's good because we're not sending data that could be compromised, so it saves us from being sniffed on the network. But if we're trying to detect what's being sent, it blocks that from our view. You have to take that into consideration. VPNs and encryption can work in our favor or they can work against us. Next we have data at rest, data sitting on a hard drive or removable media, Local to the computer or remotely on SAN or NAS storage, so that's data that's sitting there. And then we have data in use, data that's not "at rest," and only on one particular node or a network. It's being used in some fashion. It could be a memory resident piece of information, swap/temp space. We want to make sure we're protecting against all three of these categories to make sure data's not being exfiltrated or stored improperly on our network.

Next-generation Firewall (NGFW)

When it comes to firewalls, we have a general understanding of what a firewall is and what it does. But one thing you may or may not be familiar with is the concept of a next-generation firewall, or an NGFW. A next-generation firewall, they go beyond traditional firewalls and what we know a traditional firewall to do, such as stateful packet inspection or VPN services. Well, next-generation firewalls also offer advanced services like deep packet inspection, so it goes much deeper into the packet than a traditional firewall. Also, it can offer application firewalls. We can block things based on application based on the application itself, not just an IP address or a packet type? We start to move up the OSI stack. Also, things like intrusion detection and also intrusion prevention. We can do things like TLS and SSL inspection where we can decrypt packets, inspect what's inside that packet, and then send it on its way. And also, things like bandwidth management. Next-generation firewalls can combine the functionality of several different appliances or several different platforms into one device or one piece of equipment. As an example, a few next-generation firewall vendors and this is not in any specific order, and it's not an endorsement of any one product over another. I'm just giving you an idea of some of the vendors out there if you want to do a little more research on your own. We have vendors like Fortinet or Forcepoint. Also, Palo Alto Networks, SonicWall, Barracuda. Cisco also makes some next-generation firewall. Check Point advanced threat protection. Checkpoint was one of the very first VPN and firewall manufacturers out there. Also, Sophos, Juniper Networks, and the list goes on and on? These are not an exhaustive list, it's not an endorsement of one over the other. Just to give you an idea of what's out there if you want to do a little more research on your own.

HIDS/HIPS

HIDS and HIPS, host-based intrusion detection systems or intrusion prevention systems. They're similar in function to the network versions, the network intrusion detection or prevention systems; however, they run on a specific host. They don't cover an entire network. They cover a specific host. Like their network versions, they can detect anomalous behavior, and they can alert on that specific behavior. The difference is, this is a host-based, so it's running on a specific host, one system, not an entire network or a subnet or a specific part of a company. It's on a single host. When we're talking about host-based intrusion prevention systems, again, similar functionality to the network versions. They can take similar action or similar functionality to the detection systems, but they can then take action, shut down a port, run a script, do some type of workflow, in addition to alerting administrators. Very similar functionality we can run these things on a grand scale in a network environment, or we can run them specifically on individual hosts.

Host-based Firewall

When it comes to firewalls, we talked about a few different types. And in this case, we're talking about a host-based firewall. Firewalls, as we know, will typically block traffic based upon port, protocol, IP address, or perhaps application. Most server-based OSes and client-based operating systems will contain some type of virtual private networking, some type of host-based firewalls, some type of antivirus checking. You have some of these host-based tools built in to most operating systems. Then, of course, you can download free versions. You can download commercial versions. You can install enterprise-wide versions, all of which have different use cases and may fit in different environments for different reasons. But they all function generally the same way. They're going to manage and alert on some type of crossing the threshold, some type of trigger. Whether that is a port, a protocol, IP address, you can allow certain things that pass through, and you can restrict others. On host-based systems, we'll typically do that by restricting applications. You can go into that server's built-in firewall and say let these 4 or 5 or 10 or however many applications through and block everything else. Applications can be whitelisted or blacklisted. When you whitelist an application, you're saying here's the 5 or 10 or 15 applications that I'm going to allow to run. Conversely, if you say application blacklisting, you can say go ahead and run everything except for these 5 or 10 that I explicitly deny. Its two different approaches. One allows everything except what you say not to. The other one says block everything except for the 5 or 10 that I explicitly allow.

Boot Loader Protections and Secure Boot

Talking about boot loader protections, and what is a boot loader protection? Well, it's made up of a couple things here. We have secure boot; we have a measured launch; IMA, or Integrity Measurement Architecture; and then, of course, our BIOS, or UEFI, and we'll talk about each of these in more detail. Secure boot is a feature of UEFI, that allows only signed boot software to load. UEFI is Universal Extensible Firmware Interface. It's a new type of BIOS. You can think of that as the BIOS in newer systems. It allows or enables a very secure booting mechanism. If code is not signed properly, then it will halt the boot process. If we go through the steps here, firmware boot components, it's going to be digitally signed, and it's going to be digitally signed by the maker of that laptop or that piece of hardware, typically, all. It can only run certain OSs or certain boot files. It can locked down so it can only run a specific type of operating system. That firmware boot component is digitally signed, as I said it, comprised of a boot manager, again, digitally signed. It'll pass on to winload functionality, again, checks certificates, goes to the Windows kernel startup, and that will interface with the AV software initialization, and, again, checking certificates to make sure everything along the way is signed properly. That passes it back to the kernel startup, goes into additional OS initialization, passes over to boot-critical driver installation, loads our drivers, necessary to boot the system, passes it back, and then, of course, we see the windows login screen. Anywhere along that process, if those digital certificates are not on the up and up, if they've been tampered with or they're just missing, then the boot process would halt. That prevents things like root kits and pieces of malware, spyware that try to load onto the system before the actual operating system, before the antivirus software loads. If something tries to tamper in that boot sector or some type of pre-boot startup malware, this will fix that. This will prevent that from happening because it's going to alter the digital certificate. In a nutshell, when that PC starts, the firmware's going to check the signature of each piece of boot software, including firmware and drivers. If the signature's are good, the PC will boot. If not, it's going to halt that process. Not all systems have this, and you can add additional certificates in. If we have an operating system, for example, that is not included in that initial list of digital certificates, it is possible to add that in after the fact and give additional options, as far as booting that piece of equipment.

Measured Launch

Boot components have been measured, and what that means is they've been identified cryptographically. We have a hash against those things. The cryptography hashes are checked at boot to validate each component. It's part of what's called the Intel Trusted Execution Technology, or Intel TXT. And what it also does is provide a detailed log of everything that happens before the load of that actual antimalware software. If we have to go back and try to understand what happened, something got installed on our system, some piece of malware got introduced, we can go back and check this log and see exactly where that happened.

As you can imagine, it will aid in our troubleshooting and overall analysis.

Integrity Measurement Architecture (IMA)
And then next we have IMA, or Integrity Measurement Architecture. IMA is an open source alternative that creates a measured runtime environment. It creates a list of components that need to load for that operating system or for that PC to boot up. It anchors that list to what's called a TPM chip, the Trusted Platform Module. It anchors it to that chip to prevent tampering. That way, if anything changes, any type of malware tries to install and it will alter those files if they don't match, then it prevents that boot.

BIOS/UEFI
Next, we have the BIOS or UEFI, universal extensible firmware, it's an alternative to the traditional BIOS. It offers a few advantages. We can boot from disks larger than 2 TB. It's also CPU independent architecture, CPU independent drivers, so we can work whether it's on Mac, Linux, Windows system, it's not dependent upon the operating system. It's also a flexible pre-OS environment offering options of Boot menu, network boot. It gives us that secure boot environment if we need it and gives us just more options than a traditional BIOS would allow.

Hashing

Hashing is a mathematical algorithm that's applied to a file before and after transmission. If anything within that file changes, the hash will be completely different. We have a couple options, we could use MD5, SHA1, or SHA2, and that's your choice depending upon which algorithm you want to use, they will each produce a different result. In the real world, if we hashed an entire file or an entire disk, if anything has changed on that disk or in that file, depending on the example, it will result with a different hash file. Whether we're trying to send something to someone, we could take a hash first and then let them hash again when they get on the other side and see if the numbers match, if they match, we know nothing has changed, it hasn't been manipulated. Or from our forensics point of view as an example, we can take a hash of an entire hard drive, and then anytime we want to prove the veracity of that image, we can just run a hash against that again, and as long as those numbers match, we know that nothing has changed on that hard disk.

Salt

Password or passphrase salting is random data that is used as an additional input into a one-way function or hash. It defends against dictionary tax and/or rainbow table attacks. What we're doing is adding additional information to our password so that it creates an additional level of randomization, makes it harder to guess, makes it harder to bruteforce. This adds additional complexity and also makes it much more difficult to try to guess.

Secure Coding Techniques

The goal of this chapter is not to make you a very highly skilled coder. We're not deep diving into the actual nuts and bolts of coding here, but the general concepts the general mindset behind coding so that as an IT security professional you can have those conversations with the DevOps folks and with the coders and make sure that these concepts are being followed. When it comes to secure coding techniques and proper error handling. We need to make sure the errors don't crash the system, allow for elevated privileges, or expose unintended information. In having these discussions, again, with programmers and coders, understand, ask the questions, show me how error handling works. Show me what happens if unintended input is entered. What happens if the system crashes? What does it give back to the end user? Proper input validation is another. We want to make sure that we sanitize the data to mitigate such things as cross-site scripting and cross-site forgery requests. If someone goes into a web portal, we want to make sure that data is sanitized so they can't put in some rogue piece of information and get unintended results back. Also, normalization on the database back end. We want to ensure database integrity and optimization of data. You may ask yourself, what does this have to do with security? Well, normalizing the database ensures that there are no insertion or deletion anomalies. Downstream impacts might be if something gets deleted improperly or if something gets added improperly and our database and our tables are out of sync, it could return unintended consequences, or could have unintended consequences, and return unintended data, so normalization is key. Also stored procedures. We want to utilize vetted, secure procedures, verses writing new code on the fly. Whenever possible, reuse code if appropriate, or use stored procedures that have been vetted and are known to be secure. Next, we have code signing. We want to ensure that validated and trusted code is used. We want to mitigate risk from unsigned code being allowed to run. Because, again, if we allow things that have not been vetted, have not been signed, we don't know where that's coming from, we don't trust it. If we allow those things to run, we introduce risk, potential for malware, potential for spyware, ransomware, you name it, unintended results. Hackers can use these things to try to crash the system, inject code into the application. Unsigned code is a no-no.

Encrypting the data, that's going to mitigate the risk of compromise should the actual computer go missing, lost or stolen, or the drives housing the data become lost or stolen. Then we have obfuscation or camouflage. This goes hand in hand with encryption. Masking the data, encryption is an example, to avoid detection by static code analysis. That typically involves such things as a decoder and the encoded payload. You can look at these things in one of two ways. Encryption is going to keep the data out of prying eyes, but it also keeps someone from potentially reverse engineering what we're doing. If we're encrypting our code or obfuscating otherwise, camouflaging that code, they can't do static code analysis against that program and spot potential errors. It goes both ways. Those two things can either work for you or against you, depending upon which side of the fence you're sitting on. Then we have code reuse and dead code. Code reuse is simply code that can be reused, as the name implies, for some future use, future project. The challenge becomes, when people try to write code that they can reuse later, they start to bring in things that may not be necessary for the project they're working on but trying to think of future uses or future bugs they might encounter or future issues they may come up with. They try to write code that is going to counteract those things, when in reality they're probably not going to capture all those things anyway. But by focusing on what's in front of you, you stand a much better chance of writing a very clean, secure piece of code.

Server side versus client side

Take into account where validation, input sanitation, where those things occur, and the way those controls can be bypassed. Server side versus client side depends upon where those things, where those validations and those sanitizations take place. They're easier to bypass on the client side than it is on the server side, typically. Where we have the option, servicer side is typically better., not always, there's always exceptions to every rule, but just some things to think about, so the conversations to have with the coders when you're discussing how the applications work and how they function. Next is memory management. That's going to ensure that code calls and manages memory properly to avoid heap and buffer overrun errors. These things could cause the system to crash, they could cause system instability and data exposure. Things to ask your developers, making sure you're both on the same page, making sure they've thought through these things, which they may or may not have. It's always good to validate. Don't just assume that because someone works on code that they know how to do it securely. There are obvious conversations that need to be had. Then we have third-party libraries and SDKs, or software development kits. Ensure that you understand any third-party, any third-party's security requirements, their vetting processes, where their data is stored, interaction with other apps or data. Again, don't just assume that they have the same level of security that you do. Always vet that and remember that security's only as strong as the weakest link. Make sure that there is some type of service-level agreement or an understanding between companies, how they vet their process, how they take security as a consideration. Is their security up to the level of yours? Because it doesn't matter how strong your security is; if theirs is weak, then an attacker's able to come in through the side door through their weaker security and then pivot and then come through into your application or your network. That poses a challenge, and of course a breach can occur. Then, lastly we have data exposure. What types of data are exposed? If unexpected inputs are put into the system and cause the system to crash or cause some unintended result, or what errors are returned if incorrect data is entered. In other words, if someone puts in some type of string, they try a cross-site scripting or cross-site forgery request or they go through some type of fuzzing exercise or they just try every single combination of characters and letters to see what happens, to see if the system crashes. If and when it does crash, what types of information are returned? Does it tell you the operating system, the kernel version, all those things an attacker could potentially use to fingerprint the system, or if the website, as an example, asks for a username and a password, and they put in the wrong username, does it tell them, hey, this username's not valid. Well, that lets them know, hey, that one's, strike that from the list. That one's not valid. Let's try the next one. And it allows them to brute force that. Versus if it simply says, hey, if this was correct you'll get an email back or an email was sent or some type of a more ambiguous error message it doesn't give them any insight into what's valid or not valid. It's all a matter of conversations that you should have with, the coders and developers to make sure that everyone is on the same page. They will then understand how security factors in, and you will get a better understanding of how the applications interact with each other.

Chapter 3 Coding, Fuzzing & Quality Testing

We have static code analyzers; we have dynamic analysis; other words, fuzzing; we have stress testing; sandboxing; and model verification. Secure coding concepts, some things to keep in mind. Application development is often a balancing act between time to market and security. There are the developers and the general IT folks, and then there's the security folks. But we're all working on the same team, and we're all trying to do the same things, so it's important that we all work together. Building for security, that's going to add to development time. That's the general consensus, or the general understanding. But here's the key part. If you don't have time to find the vulnerabilities, guess who will? The bad guys. It's very, very important, it's crucial, in fact, that we spend the time, we do security up front, we incorporate security from the get go, not as an afterthought, not as a bolt-on. It should be done from the beginning. And the old adage is, if you don't have time to do it the first time, what makes you think you're going to have time to go back and do it a second time? If you can't do it once, how are you going to have time to do it twice? Some additional things with secure coding, error and exception handling. We need to look at what does the application do when it encounters an error? Does it continue running? Does it restart a process or a chapter? Or does it completely crash? And what type of data is exposed when it crashes? Does it give that attacker the ability to elevate privileges and get in and then do all the things that they typically would do, install persistence and go on from there, or does it give away information that tells about the type of operating system that it's on, the kernel level, some information that the attacker can use to then further dig into that system? Also input validation. It's important that we validate and sanitize what is entered at the client side or the server side, depending upon, again, your coding mechanisms and your preference. But either way, that needs to be processed and sanitized before it's passed and executed upon. That's going to allow us to mitigate attacks, cross-site scripting attacks and also SQL injection attacks, two big ones that can be avoided or mitigated if we sanitize that input properly. Metasploit, Exploit-Me, there's browser add-ons, Netsparker, there are a number of different tools out there that can allow an IT security professional to do these types of tests ahead of time. You can either throw them up to the wind and just use your best guess and hope that this stuff works and nobody tries to get in and nobody's able to get past your defenses. Or you can be proactive and use these tools and think like an attacker, think like a hacker, and start running tests against your own systems. If you don't have the expertise, bring in a pen testing team. But it's important that we test these things, we try to break things along the way so that we get to it before the attackers do.

Static Code Analysis

Static code analysis is also known as source code analysis. It's part of a code review process for something that's referred to as white-box testing, so it allows you to see under the covers. It's also part of the implementation phase of the Security Development Lifecycle or the SDL. So it finds vulnerabilities in non-running code. It's static code analysis. We're looking for those vulnerabilities, either through taint analysis or data flow analysis. Data flow analysis is used to collect runtime or dynamic information about data and software while it's in a static state. Taint analysis, on the other hand, attempts to identify variables that have been tainted by user-controllable input and then traces that to possible vulnerable functions also known as a sink. If a tainted variable gets past to a sink without first being sanitized, it gets flagged as a vulnerability. We're looking for vulnerabilities, we're looking for input sanitization, looking for places where a user has the ability to control that input. If they can put in something, this is where SQL injection and cross-site scripting attacks come into play. If they're able to use some type of technique either as fuzzing or just straight up SQL injection, they can try every single possible combination of codes, letters, characters, and if that is successful, and that code does not get sanitized, they can crash the system or have unintended results. This data flow analysis and this taint analysis allows us to go in and identify these things ahead of time. It's part of the defensive posture that we need to take as IT security professionals, does every IT security professional know all of these different things? No, of course not. There are areas of specialization, but it's important for you to have a general concept and a general understanding, number one, to know, is this an area I want to go into, number two, even if it isn't, you need to have those conversations with the people that are responsible for this, and if you don't know about it, it's hard to have that conversation. As an IT security professional, it's important to have a good understanding of everything, not a deep dive, but a good understanding, so you know who to talk to, who to coordinate with, whether they're developers, pen testers, coders, your DevOps folks, or IT security folks, your infrastructure folks, all the different lines of business, you can reach out to all these different areas, coordinate efforts, and make sure everyone is on the same page and everyone is working towards the same goal.

Fuzzing

Fuzzing is intentionally trying to crash a program or an application by providing invalid, unexpected or random data. Fuzzing is a set of tools. It's not a specific application, it's a suite of applications. It can be one or a dozen or more. Each hacker, each attacker, each forensics person, they all have their own toolsets that they like to work with. It's used by application designers and testers internally, as well as hackers on the outside, but if we're going to use it internally, it helps us to find bugs and defects, also security holes in our applications. It allows us to identify things we didn't account for. Hackers, they'll use fuzzing techniques as well. They'll look for zero-day vulnerabilities, and a lot of hackers will go out there and they'll gather up these zero-days and they'll sell them on the dark net, they'll hoard them, sell them to companies, sell them to security companies or perhaps rogue states or nation states. There are three-letter agencies within the U.S. government that buy these zero-day vulnerabilities from various hackers, so they'll hoard them as well. And then these hackers will also sell them to the bad guys. It's a very effective toolset, it can yield some great results, it can be used for good or bad, but it's important for us to use those same techniques to identify things internally. Whether we're trying to crash applications or websites, we want to make sure we get to our vulnerabilities before the bad guys do. There are a few fuzzing applications out there. One that makes it easy for you, there's a Linux distribution called Kali Linux. They have a suite of fuzzing tools built in, al. Also, CERT has one called BFF, or the Basic Fuzzing Framework, that you can download from the web link, and that allows you to bring in a full suite of fuzzing applications. Whether you go Linux distribution or you download a framework ahead of time, it allows you to install and use the same types of tools that these hackers use. I urge you to become proficient in what these things do, or at least develop on your team someone who is proficient in this so that you can then coordinate their efforts.

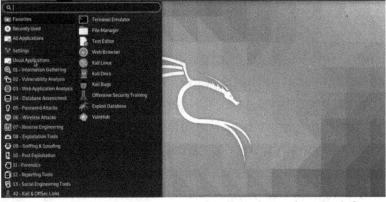

Here we have Kali Linux, which I downloaded from their website, and I'll bring up their actual web page within the actual VM that I'm running here. This is a virtual machine, so it's a little bit slower than it normally would be, but if you were to go out to

Kali's website, which is kali.org, this is a reincarnation of BackTrack, which is a pen testing tool and a Linux distribution that's geared towards security. If you're familiar with BackTrack, this is the newer version of that toolset, so Kali Linux. And from there you would go to Downloads. If you're running VMware, this is a great way to get up and running quickly. You click on that and it will bring you over to this web page from Offensive Security, and then from there you can download custom ARM images and also VMware images. You would just pick one for your specific VMware flavor of choice, and from there, once you install it, which is what I have running here, you're up and running with Kali Linux and you can explore all the things that it has to offer. Under Applications down under Kali Linux, this is where all the good stuff, this is where all the magic happens. It's out of the scope of this book to go into any of these in any depth, but I wanted to make you aware of where they're located and how to get your hands on a copy of Kali Linux You can explore on your own. From the fuzzing testing tools that I was referring to, that would be under Vulnerability Analysis and then down under Fuzzing Tools.

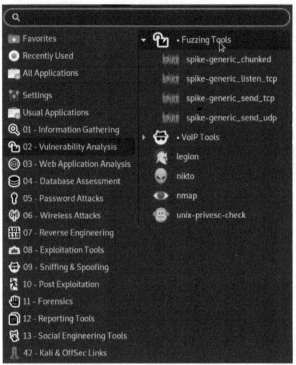

You see there's a number of ones available. There's also Database Assessment tools, Reverse Engineering, Stress Testing, Exploitation Tools, so there's a lot of stuff here, If you're interested in digging in, I highly recommend that you download this application, or this distribution of Linux, and then start exploring the applications that are inside here, so I just want to make you aware of where these things were located.

Additional Secure Coding Concepts
Stress testing is placing load on the system or the application. We want to see where the performance

and the usability breaks down, where that application either crashes or simply can't perform anymore. We can test via automated processes with like LoadRunner or Iometer or use some type of appliance like a load dynamics device, some piece of hardware, and we can stress test whether it's an array, whether it's an application, a server. We can see where things fall apart. We can turn up the number of users, the number of connections, the number of processes that's being processed at once. We do that to simulate where is that going to break down in the real world. If we have 5 users, it's great. If we have 500, it's a little iffy. If we have 5000, it falls apart. Well, we need to know that ahead of time, before we put into production. We put an ad on TV and all of a sudden we have 10,000 users trying to hit our website at the same time or hit our application at the same time, and it falls apart. It's not good for our reputation or for consumer confidence. Not to mention, if it doesn't fail gracefully, it could expose information and be a security risk. Next, we have sandboxing. Sandboxing is isolating the application from other systems so that we can test without impact to other applications to production. We've talked about a few ways to sandbox. We can isolate the networks logically or physically, we can use VMware or some other type of hypervisor and virtualize that environment. It allows us to just as segment that off from the rest. And then we have model verification. This is testing to verify that the product or the application that's produced aligns with the proposed model. Does it do what we said it's going to do? Does it behave in the way that we thought it's going to behave? Because it's possible to build something that's going to behave or interact with other systems that's totally different from what you thought it was going to do. Model verification is critical to make sure all the boxes are checked and make sure that we understand all the downstream impacts and how this specific application or this specific system interacts with everything else that's in production.

Peripherals Security

Peripheral security is something we typically think of, a mouse or a keyboard, what's the harm? Well, wireless keyboards, wireless mice, all of those things can be sniffed potentially. The average environment, maybe not a big deal, but depending upon how critical your infrastructure is or how crucial your job function or the industry you're in, all of those things are attack vectors, so they need to be considered, Wireless keyboards, wireless mice, displays, we've talked about emanations from displays before, such things as TEMPEST-proof rooms, Faraday cages. Also, Wi-Fi-enabled MicroSD cards, we have a camera digital device, a lot of those things days have Wi-Fi-enabled SD cards, you can upload pictures and data from that SD card directly. Well, all of those things are potentially open for compromise. Hackers are getting into everything, embedded systems, Internet of Things, even cars on the highway. It's important to always understand that every single thing in our environment is a potential attack surface, we need to remove things we don't need, and then the things that are left, we need to make sure we monitor, update, and patch. Same thing goes with printers and MFDs, the multi-function devices, external storage devices, and digital cameras. All of these things contain data that, if not either removed or strictly controlled, the access is strictly controlled, data can be pulled off of those devices if they're accessed or if they're compromised. When we talk about updating, just the overall peripheral security, a few things we should be doing, some common-sense things, and that is update and patch. We need to make sure we keep all of our systems and all the peripherals patched and updated. Just because it's an embedded system, or an appliance, doesn't mean it shouldn't be monitored, patched, and updated. Then we need to make sure we physically secure devices. Treat peripherals like any other asset. They could contain sensitive data, so don't let things walk out the door. Make sure you have an eye on things in a way to monitor, whether it's barcodes or sensors or what have you, make sure we can keep an eye on all of our assets. And then, require credentials to access, Printers or copiers, and don't just let anyone access your resources. Make sure they have to badge in or put in some type of access code so that way you can monitor who is using those resources. Last but not least, we should definitely require encryption of removable devices, external storage, or Wi-Fi connectivity, whenever possible. All of these things combine to help to strengthen our security posture and mitigate risks as much as possible.

Hardening the Environment
When we're talking about hardening the environment, I'm talking about open ports and services, locking things down that we don't need, and making sure that it is secure as it can possibly be, and still be useful. There is a fine line, you can lock things down much to the point where it's not useful anymore or people have to write down passwords, usernames and have sticky notes everywhere. It is possible to overdo it, but in this instance, let's talk about what we can do proactively to harden the environment. When you build your systems, your servers, desktops, even mobile devices, develop the mindset to do an analysis of the environment, of that application, of that device and see there are a lot of things there that we don't

need. We can turn those things off. It's never going to do X, Y, Z, so we don't need to have that service listening, we don't need to have that service active because as we remove or disable services, shut down ports, we're doing what? We're shrinking the attack service. So open ports and services is one and there are things within the registry, and the registry in a Windows system at least, is sort of like the DNA of the system, it has all the fine-grained controls, it allows you to shut certain things off and make things harder to access or just disable services. Disk encryption we've talked about before as well. We need to make sure we're covering our bases. And if, in fact, a piece of equipment gets stolen, removed out of a car, out of the data center, out of a storage closet, and if the disk is encrypted, it's going to be much more difficult for that bad actor to access the information on that disk. And then OS hardening, just like we talked about with open ports and services, we want to remove unnecessary services at the OS level as well, shut down things that aren't necessary, remote desktop protocol, as an example, there are many more, but that's just one. If we don't need it, then shut it off. That removes that ability or shrinks that attack service. Next is patch management. We need to make sure that we do that religiously, and that goes for third-party updates and also auto update. Auto update may or may not be something you want to do in your environment and larger environments. We want to do things on a cadence. We want to be able to download those updates offline, test them in a very small group, do some regression testing, make sure they don't break anything, and then roll them out systematically to the environment at large. That way it gives you the opportunity to phase things in, and that way you don't just automatically update something and have a break. It's not to say you can't automate the process, but you just don't want to automate patching without testing it first.

Common Ports

When we talk about ports and services, there are things called common ports. It's beyond the scope of this book to go into all of the reports. There are over 65,500 ports. The first 1,024 are defined by RFC or request for comments, and they're known as the well-known ports. They're defined by typical applications. But these are some of the ones that you should be familiar with, port 20 and 21 for FTP as an example, port 23 for Telnet. Here's an example of one you may or may not need. If you don't need to Telnet your service or into your server or your desktop, then disable that service. It just shrinks that attack surface. If you go down the list and look at things like, as an example, Internet Relay Chat, port 194. Well, this isn't 1985. People don't use IRC anymore. If you need in your environment, great. Keep it up. But if you don't, block those things at the firewall. Block those things at the individual host as well. By doing so, we're removing or at least shrinking the attack surface. Is it foolproof? No. But why give attackers or bad actors more fuel for their fire, more ammunition. Shrink it as much as possible; help to make things more secure.

Registry Hardening

When we talk about registry hardening, registry being the DNA of the operating system, at least on the Windows side. An example of some registry hardening settings, configure permissions, deny anonymous access as an example. Deny remote registry access as an example. If you need that in your environment, then by all means don't do that, but this where it comes down to an analysis of each individual environment. Everyone's going to have different needs. Everyone's going to have different working parameters or guidelines or guardrails that they have to operate within. Make sure that you configure your permissions appropriately. But make them as restrictive as possible and still being useful. Also, I would disable access to registry editing tools at the host level as well. That way, someone can't go in at the host and start editing the registry. That goes for disabling the command prompt and also PowerShell access if it's not needed. There might be instances where you do need that, and if so, then by all means keep it enabled. But by doing that, by making people local users on the machines, taking away access to certain things that allow them to bypass some of the controls you're putting in place, it makes the system more secure. It reduces your troubleshooting and shrinks the attack surface. And then Whitelist and blacklist applications. The difference between whitelisting and blacklisting. Whitelisting is we have a list of acceptable applications. Everything else is no go. If you only have three applications on that list, then they're the only three things that we can run. Conversely, if you have a blacklist, we can run everything except the ones that are on the blacklist. It's just two different approaches to achieve the same net effect.

Self-encrypting Drives (SED)

Self-encrypting drives, also known as SED drives. These things are very much like a typical disk drive, except they have additional functionality. They can self encrypt and they maintain that information on the disk itself, so you don't need to maintain third-party encryption keys. Encryption keys are self-contained in the drive's firmware, and they're maintained separately from the CPU, which, again, reduces the attack vector. That's the name of the game here. We want to shrink the attack vector as much as possible. There's something else that I want to make you aware of, and that is the Opal Specification, and that deals with self-encrypting drives. It was created by the Trusted Computing Group, or TCG, and it's a security subsystem class that specifies how data is encrypted on the drive. If we look at this in a little more detail, this is a very high-level overview of how it works. But you have your host interface in which you input plain text, you have your plain text that you want to encrypt onto the storage device. We have what's called a KDF, or a key derivation function. That's how we're going to create the key-encrypting key, the KEK. That key-encrypting key, usually a password, an authentication PIN here or a password, is then used to create what's called the MEK, or the media encryption key. We're taking a key, a master key, if you will. It then unlocks the media encryption keys and allows that data to be unencrypted or encrypted, depending on which way it's going in, whether you're writing it or reading it from disk. You don't need to necessarily understand the nitty-gritty of how it works, but just understand at a high level that self-encrypting drives are secure. They're a little more secure in the fact that we don't have to maintain third-party encryption keys. They're also more efficient in that we don't have to worry about the CPU or burdening the CPU with additional cycles to have the software or a software layer encrypt and decrypt the data. It's handled at the actual drive level, and those keys are stored in the firmware. That makes it very secure. It gives you very good throughput and takes that latency out of the process of the software layer, having to do the encryption and decryption, which puts additional cycles onto the CPU. By removing all of that, we make the encryption process more streamlined.

Hardware Root of Trust

Next, we have a concept referred to as the hardware root of trust. What does this mean? Well, you can see that it goes up the stack from the hardware to firmware, Hypervisor, operating system, up to the application, and what that means is that root of trust begins with systems that are inherently trusted, just like we have PKI and we have certificate authorities and root certificate authorities, that same level of trust needs to be there. If something is compromised at the very low level at the base hardware, if the BIOS of a system are compromised, then how can we trust anything that sits above that? If the BIOS itself is not inherently trusted or inherently secure, then we can trust as we go up that stack and test that the other things in that stack can be secure as well. A few concepts regarding that hardware root of trust, it needs to be secure by design, it also needs to perform security-critical functions like the TPM chip, as we mentioned, as an example, or boot firmware is another example. There are two NIST guidelines I'd like to call your attention to, NIST SP800-147, which is BIOS protection guidelines, and then NIST SP600-155 which is BIOS integrity measurement guidelines. Those two guidelines I encourage you to download and look through. They'll give you some additional information around the general concept and how that applies within your organization.

Hardware Based Encryption
Next up, and a few things that you should be aware of here, TPM being one of them, the Trusted Platform Module and TPM is a hardware chip that's embedded on a computer's motherboard. Typically, you're going to see these in laptops. They're used to store cryptographic keys used for encryption. The TPM chapter is built onto a motherboard. The takeaway here is it cannot be added later. If your desktop or your laptop or whatever the device is does not have a TPM chip, you cannot add it later. It's built into the motherboard itself. Conversely, we have HSM, or the hardware security Module. It functions in much the same way as a TPM; however, this can be external, or it could be plugged into a server or a laptop. It is something that can be added later. Imagine that we have a network device, a network-based hardware security chapter, and this is used for storing and generating

keys for encryption. Whether you have a PKI on your network or you're looking for some type of encryption technology, this can do that at the network level. There's also cards that can be plugged in to a specific server. HSM, the takeaway would be it's similar to TPM. The hardware security chapter is very similar to the Trusted Platform Chapter; however, HSMs are removable or they're external. They can be added later. That's the takeaway. TPMs are built in, HSMs are not. Both are used, however, for encryption keys, encrypting rather, and using RSA keys. Next, we have USB encryption. For the most part, when we say removable media, we're talking about USB or thumb drives. It's the same type of thing. Encrypting the contents of our USB drives, it prevents that data from being accessed if stolen, or if someone maliciously tries to copy data onto a USB drive and hand it off to someone else, that data's encrypted. The receiving party can't do much with it unless they have those decryption keys. Then we have hardware-based encryption around hard drives. Encrypting the entire contents of a hard drive, that provides that data at rest encryption, and it guards against data leakage if lost or stolen. Again, someone smashes the window or breaks into a place of business and steals computers, steals laptops, that data is inaccessible. It's also used in conjunction with the TPM or HSM chapters. These things help generate the encryption keys in a very secure environment. That way, if it gets lost or stolen, there's not much you can do with it. As an example, we have BitLocker. This would give us an entire or full disk encryption. We can turn on, go into our control panel, and turn on BitLocker at the drive level, where we have multiple drives, and ensure that those things are encrypted and, of course, inaccessible if they were to be either stolen or fall into the wrong hands.

Sandboxing

Sandboxing can be used in a couple of different contexts. In this specific context, it's isolating code, upgrades, and testing from the production environment. In other words, we're operating in a closed or a walled garden, so we can test changes, and we can do things without affecting production. We can do such things as test code changes, we can roll back changes very quickly, we can also regression test against various applications, or execute and even observe malware. We can purposely allow malware to do its thing, but it's in a sandboxed environment, we're observing it, trying to reverse engineer it, or at least see what it's doing, what's the payload? Sandboxing in an environment allows us to put those walls up and operate safely. When we're talking about sandboxing applications, it isolates the application from other user data, resources, you can think of it as virtual environments within your device, a mobile device, laptop or desktop. It can prevent malware and viruses from interacting with the application or with other applications, and each application has its own environment on the host. That prevents an application crash from affecting other applications running on the host. It's not anything that's revolutionary, but it is a tried-and-true practice that allows us to operate securely without affecting other applications. And we can do it sandbox from a network perspective, we can do it from an application perspective, we can do it to test code and roll back changes, or we can create live environments that each application can live in on a specific device, separating those applications from each other. In this chapter, we covered endpoint protection; we talked about boot integrity; and database security; along with application security, hardening, and the importance of doing that around ports and services, the registry, OS; we talked about disk encryption; we talked about the hardware root of trust, along with a Trusted Platform Module; and then we also talked about sandboxing in a few different contexts.

Chapter 4 How to Implement Secure Network Designs

In this chapter, we'll be talking about Implementing Secure Network Designs and we'll be covering such things as load balancing, we'll be talking about network segmentation, we'll talk about virtual private networks, DNS or domain name service, we'll also talk about network access control or NAC, also out-of-band management, and then wrap up with port security. A load balancer, as the name implies, balances the load between devices. A load balancer can be put in place in a number of areas. It could be a server. There could be other devices as well. It can be hardware. It can be software. It just depends upon price point, functionality, how extreme the load balancing needs to be. If it's a small environment, a server may be fine. If it's a large environment, very high volume, then you're going to need a dedicated appliance. If we have a number of users, there's the external network, and then there's a load balancer in place, and it can be one or more. It doesn't necessarily have to be a single device. It could be multiple load balancers. In this instance, let's just say we have web servers, and it's going to balance the load and determine, which is the best performing server at that specific point in time, and I'm going to send the load to that server.

It may go in a round-robin fashion. It may use some algorithm to determine, but depending upon the load balancer itself, it's going to determine in some fashion, which is the best server or the best device to send that load to. It allows you to spread it out across. And as a load starts to pick up, as websites become more busy, it can spread it out so that no one server gets completely overwhelmed. A few terms I want to make sure you're familiar with regard to load balancers. As far as scheduling is concerned, we have two terms, affinity and round-robin. Affinity means if we have multiple servers, that a load balancer can serve traffic too. Well, if it has affinity in place, then the server that initially serviced the request for a host, it will use that same server for the entirety of that session. It's not going to just completely just go to the next available one. It locks into that server, and as long as that session is active, that post will communicate over that load balancer into that server, so the host to server will take the same path through the load balancer. In a round-robin fashion, we may have multiple load balancers. We may have multiple servers to get through to the back-end database or the back-end application. While in a round-robin fashion, it will pick the next available or the next best one in line, It won't necessarily wait or lock into a specific server and hold communication throughout the entirety of that session. It will go to the next available one. When we're talking about active-passive dealing with load balancers, that refers to the fact that we may have multiple load balancers. Even load balances have load balancers. The load balancer itself is operating in an HA or a highly-available fashion. The active-passive nature means one load balancer is handling or servicing all that traffic. There's another load balancer that's acting in a passive state, and it's monitoring what the first load balancer's doing. It's keeping track, but it's not doing anything. It's not actively servicing requests. Its job is to jump in in case the primary load balancer were to go offline or have some type of failure. In an active-active capacity, we have both load balancers servicing the load or it might have multiple, three or four, however many are in this configuration. But for this example, let's say we have two load balancers. Well, if they're acting in an active-active fashion, they're both servicing the load, spreading it evenly. The downside of that is in an active-active situation, both load balancers end up servicing requests near their maximum capacity. If one load balancer were to go down and there's no other load balancer to take over, then we'll start slowing down and customers will notice a degradation in service. In an active-passive fashion, one load balancer is servicing everything. If it starts to go down, the other one kicks in and takes over, so there's no noticeable difference, no noticeable degradation to end users. And then the last one I want to cover is virtual IPs. A virtual IP, or a VIP, is an IP that sits in front of all of the actual IPs that the load balancers use, so that way the end user doesn't necessarily need to know the IP addresses of the individual load balancers. All they need to know is the one, and it will cycle through and make sure that it goes to the proper load balancers behind the scenes. That way you don't have to change things. If you add additional load balancers or you switch things up behind the scenes, end users, all they need to know is they have to connect to that virtual IP address.

Security Segmentation Models

Let's now talk about segregation, segmentation and isolation. We have a few security or segmentation models I want to call to your attention. First is physical. We can physically separate or segment nodes or hosts on a network. We can also do that logically with something called VLAN, or virtual LANs, virtual local area networks. We can also do it with virtualization, so an isolation model or a segmentation model. Then we also have air gapped, meaning there is no connectivity to the internet or to the network at large. So, what do I mean by that? Well, with physical or logical, we have devices that are all on the same segment, the same Ethernet segment or the same LAN, the same local area network. And in this example, you can assume that they're all connected to the same switch, so that is a physical connectivity to the network. Well, we can also logically separate those networks. We can take that same layout, but we can use something called virtual LANs, or virtual local area networks, and group them accordingly. We can have a VLAN10, we can have a VLAN20, and in this case, a VLAN30. What that does is separate those devices out. What it does is create separate broadcast domains, separate security domains, and it reduces the chatter. Let's look at another example. Imagine that we have a multi-floor building. We have wiring on each floor that goes back to a home run, and it goes down between floors. We have devices on the first floor and a switch, we have devices on the second floor and a switch, and then devices on the third floor and a switch. It's not the only way to wire, not the only way to do it, but in this example, we have each floor going to a wiring closet. In that wiring closet, a switch, and then those switches are connected via home runs. They're all physically located in different locations. Well, we can also group those together just like we did in the previous example. They don't have to be sitting next to each other. We can group them again logically, VLAN10, VLAN20, and then VLAN30. In other words, if we had groups of computers that may be on different floors, let's say we have finance people that sit on all three floors or HR or our graphics department we can group them within our switches. We make sure that all the switches have the same VLAN associations, and that way they're grouped logically together. Those VLANs can group hosts that are in different locations, into logical groupings. That creates smaller collision domains and it reduces chatter. As an example, if you have a very large cafeteria, everyone's talking. It's very hard to understand because everyone's talking. Everyone's clashing into each other. They're colliding the conversations. If I took all of those people in that cafeteria and separated them out into five different rooms or in this example three different rooms, well, I have one third of the amount of people in each room, so the chatter is going to be less, so the collisions are less. It helps increase efficiency. Then also it can be used to create security boundaries to segment traffic so that one host doesn't necessarily see broadcasts and doesn't see traffic designated for hosts in another VLAN.

Virtualization

Virtualization is a method of segmenting or isolating, so we can keep a host in a sandboxed and isolated environment, meaning it's separate from the host that it's sitting on. We can also allow for snapshots. We can quickly revert changes, we can use virtualization to isolate or segment. We can do all of our testing. We can test changes, we can even test viruses or malware to see what it does without affecting the rest of the network and without affecting the host that it sits on. It also separates the guests from the host, the guest from the hypervisor. If we have Hyper-V, or VMware, or KVM, or virtual box, or whatever the case might be or whatever our virtualization technology is, this allows us to keep those individual guests separate from the host. Other devices may be virtualized as well. We can virtualize other infrastructure, such as routers, switches, load balancers, firewalls, and we'll talk more about that when we get into SDN, but the nice part is those things can be instantiated or spun up on demand, so as a load increases, we could spin up additional load balancers or, if we have applications that need specific firewalls, instead of having to go through the normal change process and buying equipment and racking and stacking and all the things that are associated with physical infrastructure, we can do it virtually, very quickly, spin that device up, use it while we need it, and then we can tear it down just as quickly.

Air Gaps
An air gap is a method of isolating a computer or a network from the internet or from other external networks, or other networks aside from the one you're on. So, it doesn't necessarily have to be just

from the internet, it could be from other networks within your company. If you have a very highly secure environment that you need to make sure that there's no chance of malware or viruses being introduced, then you would set up an air gapped network. As with anything, there is no 100% guarantee, as we've seen in the past with things like Stuxnet and some other very highly visible and highly cited instances where malware has jumped into air gapped environments, nothing is 100% certain. But it's used for critical infrastructure, SCADA systems, as an example, and I refer back to Stuxnet where the SCADA systems were still compromised, highly secure classified networks. There are some advanced techniques, however, to jump air gapped networks, like I said, that's been demonstrated, emanations, there's technology and it's been completely demonstrated where they can view the emanations coming off of a computer, whether it is the sound of the hard drive whirring, or even the heat being generated by the hard drive spinning up. If you're close enough to that device, you can pick those things up from the device and discern what's going on, you can read data from that device. Pretty advanced stuff and it's not something the average hacker can do, but just understand that an air gap is a very good way of isolating the network, but it's not 100% foolproof. In fact, the US government and other agencies around the world have specific guidelines to create additional security. The US uses something referred to as TEMPEST, which protects that room, it has to be a certain thickness of walls and has to have additional coding and protections, Faraday cages, and things that just prevent emanations and monitoring from nearby locations. Emanations, FM frequencies, even some hard drives that have a small LED light on the front that shows activity of that drive, you don't see that too much anymore, but it is possible that if you have a line of sight visibility to that light going on and off as the hard drive writes, you could read, almost like Morse is code, what's going on with that hard drive and read data from that device. Pretty scary, but the average hacker is not going to be employing that. More than likely, you can rest assured that your home network is safe.

East-west Traffic

East-West traffic is data moving between devices within a data center. More and more traffic is being generated days East-West, just as a side note, with less and less traffic going North-South, meaning entering or exiting the data center. Again, depending upon your data center in your company, you may refer to North-South traffic as traffic leaving the top of rack and going to another area within the data center. Sometimes terminology can be co-mingled depending upon the company, the data center, but generally speaking, East-West is within the data center, North-South is exiting or entering the data center. Traditional firewalls and monitoring look normally or traditionally at North-South traffic. Our firewalls are on our perimeter, and we want to guard against what's coming into our networks and what's leaving the networks. That lack of visibility can add to an attacker's ability to move laterally around in a network undetected. Once they get into the network, once they penetrate our defenses, there's normally not as much tooling and not as much visibility into the movement within the data center, the thought being that once you're inside the network, it's a trusted environment. We'll talk more about zero trust in just a moment, but understand that that lack of visibility can allow an attacker to move around virtually undetected, at least for a period of time. How do we combat that is we implement network monitoring to identify that East-West threat or the East-West traffic. An IDS, or an IPS, or a network IDS, or network IPS system combined with tools like Suricata or Zeek, again two open-source recommendations, not the only things out there and not an endorsement, just giving you some ideas of things to look at, but Suricata and Zeek can identify malicious activity and can integrate with other systems as well, again these intrusion detection and prevention systems, and they can be leveraged to identify that malicious activity and take steps to mitigate it.

Zero Trust

Keeping with that theme, let's talk about zero trust, which I mentioned just a moment ago. Zero trust in today's world, castle moat philosophy where everything behind the firewalls was thought to be safe is no longer valid. That is not the recommended way to do things anymore. We need to take a more granular approach. Internal and external traffic should be monitored nothing implicitly trusted, whether it's internal or external. Micro-segmentation and granular access, providing only the levels of permission required. In other words, we don't just assume if you're inside the network, you're good, go ahead, don't necessarily worry about it. As we talked about, that allows an attacker to go around and move around, laterally jump networks, peruse the parking lot, and see which car they want to steal. We don't want that. That micro-segmentation, granular access, locking things down to only give people the level of permissions required, which sounds familiar. We do that anyway, typically with ACLs on resources like file shares, but we also want to make sure that we do it at the resource level, the servers, the storage arrays, data protection, so on. A couple of tools we can leverage would be MFA, or multi-factor authentication, IAM, identity access management, and then we can leverage orchestration and analytics along with encryption. All of these more modern toolsets and these technologies, combined with detection and prevention tools, can lock down the environment enough so that it's not an easy target for an attacker or a bad actor, but we still need to make it usable, for our internal users. It's a fine line, but just understand the old way of doing things is not applicable or should not be applicable in today's environment.

VPN
The next thing I want to talk about is a VPN, or a virtual private network. A VPN is going to be something you should probably be familiar with. But if not, I'll give you a very good understanding here and the general concepts of what a VPN does. A VPN creates a virtual private network across a public network. You could be sitting in a coffee shop, for instance, very securely tunnel from that coffee shop to your corporate environment and access corporate resources without worrying that someone is potentially sniffing the traffic, accessing or picking up a sense of information like usernames, passwords. There are a couple of components of a VPN that we need to be aware of. Tunneling protocols such as L2TP, or Layer 2 Tunneling

Protocol, and also PPTP, Point-To-Point Tunneling Protocol, and then IPSec, or IP security. What do these things mean? Well, there are separate components that make up the VPN because there are two components that we need to talk about. There's the tunnel, and then there's the encrypted data that passes through the tunnel. When we're establishing a VPN connection, the first thing we do is establish the tunnel, and then you establish the secure connection or the encrypted connection between the two endpoints. Security comes from the tunneling protocol and the encryption combined, and that's very important to understand. You can't have security unless you have both of those things in play. You need to establish the tunnel and then establish the security with encryption that passes data through that tunnel. Just because you have a tunnel established, if you don't have the encrypted communication taking place over that tunnel, then it's not going to do you much good as far as security is concerned. Many VPNs use something referred to as two-factor authentication. RSA is a very good example of that. They're one of the bigger vendors recently acquired by EMC. And RSA can provide hardware and software tokens, and what happens is every 30 seconds, or so, the number on that token or that Django, as it's called, will change. That number is in sync with the VPN concentrator or the VPN server back at the corporate headquarters, back at the endpoint. There's an authentication mechanism that keeps both of these in sync. Every 30 seconds that number changes on both the endpoint and also on the token. When you go to establish your connection, it's going to ask you for that username and perhaps your PIN or a password if you're going to use something like an RSA token. It will ask you for that. You have two things, what you have and what you know. You know your username and the token is what you have. That's going to change every 30 seconds, making it much more secure. Even if someone steals your laptop and they know your username, they still won't be able to gain access or get into a VPN connection and get back to the corporate headquarters because they don't have what? They don't have that PIN or that token that changes every 30 seconds. They're going to have to physically take that RSA token as well. Then even if they have the RSA token, they'll still need to know your PIN because once you put your PIN in, then, of course, the token will pop up. It's an extra layer of added security. With VPNs, many companies provide VPN access to their remote employees, so it allows corporate access to resources from an offsite or remote location. Depending on how things are set up, it can be given complete access to the network. Once you VPN in, once you make that connection, you could have complete access to the corporate network, or access can be restricted to only certain parts of the network. Depending upon how that VPN administrator sets things up, a person dialing in or VPN-ing into the network can have access maybe to only a certain subnet or a certain set of files and folders, a certain server. Here's an example of two different types of VPN connections. We have a VPN connection between two corporate networks, and it's a VPN connection in a tunnel, and you have a VPN router on both networks? Pretty much in these instances, a lot of times, it's set up as a constant connection, and then we have a VPN connection from a remote user. In this instance, that user is sitting out on the internet, again some public network. It could be a home office or remote office, some coffee shop somewhere. In other words, it's somewhere outside of the corporate environment proper. That person connects to their ISP. Now they have internet connectivity. When they initiate that VPN connection, it connects them to the corporate environment. They establish the VPN connection, the tunnel, and then the communication is secured over the public internet. They don't have to worry about someone being able to sniff their traffic.

Split Tunnel
In a split tunnel situation, we have an outside or an external user who is external to the company

network or the corporate network. Imagine that we have our 10.x network that's our internal corporate network. The user who is sitting external, maybe their home, at a coffee shop, some remote location. While they want to access those corporate resources, but as a company, it doesn't make sense to have that user go into our corporate network and then back out again to access external resources. So by using a split tunnel, we make sure that that external user accesses our corporate resources over the VPN so they have secure access to company resources, but then, when they want to reach external resources, they do Directly without going through the corporate network.

IPSec and Transport Encryption
Next, we have something referred to as IPSec, or the internet security protocol, and this allows us to encrypt communication over the internet over that insecure or unsecured network. There is two components here we have an authentication header, an AH, that provides authentication and integrity that does not encrypt the data, it just allows you to prove that you're communicating with who you think you're communicating with and that the data has not been manipulated or somehow tweaked while in transit, someone then pulled off the wire, manipulated it, and put it back on, so it proves authentication and integrity. We have the

original IP header, the TCP section, and the payload. This is a data packet. What we're doing is adding an authentication header. No encryption as the AH only offers integrity, so it proves authentication and integrity. If we want to encrypt that data, then we're going to need something referred to as the encapsulating secure payload, or ESP. That provides also confidentiality, along with optional integrity checking, so it adds a header, a trailer, and an integrity check value, or an ICV, so that works as such. So now we have that data packet, the original header, we're going to add in an ESP header, the encapsulating secure payload, TCP is the transport protocol, the actual payload, which is the data that we're sending, it's going to an ESP trailer and ESP authentication, so that's going to give us a fully secure data pack as it traverses over that unsecure medium, and that's encrypted, which provides data confidentiality.

VPN Concentrator
We've talked about VPN several times before, but in this specific instance, we're talking about a VPN concentrator, and that has the ability to create large numbers of VPN tunnels. It's not just a single tunnel, a single point to point. A concentrator can do numerous tunnels, typically used for site-to-site architectures. In this example here, we have a site-to-site VPN, and we have two networks? We

have a secure network on one side, a secure network on the other side, and in that tunnel, we have multiple VPN connections going through that tunnel, because we have VPN routers that are concentrators on either side of that tunnel. Conversely, we have a remote access VPN where we have a single person, maybe a remote teleworker or a very small office where we have one person or a single tunnel going from that remote location into the corporate internet. You'll still have a VPN concentrator on the one side, but then you have an ISP being used from the guest or the host or the small office on the other side, and they'll be going through that VPN tunnel. It's a concentrator, because even though that specific location may only have one tunnel going through, you may have multiple remote locations. So it has the ability to create multiple tunnels at once.

Chapter 5 Network Access Control, Port Security & Loop Protection

NAC or Network Access Control or Network Admission Control, depending upon, where you read or what context it's being used in, it refers to a set of policies that define a minimal set of requirements each device must have before being allowed on the network. We want to make sure that if someone pulls out their laptop and tries to connect to our network, it's going to check and say, hey, do you have this level of firmware, do you have this level of virus or anti-virus patching, do you have, all these different required security patches maybe for the OS, and if you don't, well, we're not going to let you on the network, so it does a check before it allows that access. This becomes more and more important as BYO devices become prevalent within the environment, people bring their own laptops or their own mobile phones. A couple applications that can help with that, I'm just giving you some examples, Good Messaging, Mobile Iron, and Airwatch are three mobile device management tools, or MDMs, that allow us to make sure that those devices are in compliance before they're allowed to connect to the network. Devices can be denied access, or they can be placed in what's called a secure zone until those minimum requirements are met. It may give them a cordoned-off area and says, you can connect to our network in this little safe space, and from there you can download the required patches or the required security fixes, applications, and until you do that, you can't go anywhere else. It gives them a chance to remediate the issue. Once those things are done, it will check again, and if they meet compliance, then they're allowed onto the network. Network Access Control can also be implemented in one of three ways. We have what's called a permanent agent, and that's persistent, that's persistently installed on the host device, and runs continuously. From an enterprise perspective, this is the best option, because we know for a fact that it's installed on that device we can tell what's going on all the time. From the end user perspective, they may or may not want that, especially if it's a BYO device. They may say, I don't want someone snooping on my device or potentially, pulling data off that I don't know about. Well, that's a choice you have to make within your own environment, but permanent agents are typically preferred at an enterprise level. And then we have a dissolvable agent. This is one that runs in a portal. A user will connect, it will download the agent, and it's going to run once. It will then disappear. If they need to use it again, it can be either re-downloaded or it can be fired back up again, but it doesn't run continuously in the background. Then we have agentless, which can come in a few different forms. In this instance, it's embedded within Active Directory, and that NAC code verifies that the host complies with access policies, typically when they join a domain, when they log on or when they log off. Normally it will trigger and will run or scan that device when one of those three things happen.

In-band vs. Out-of-band Management
Network devices can be managed and access both in-band and also out-of-band, depending upon preference, architectural decisions or limitations. In-band means traffic can be examined in real time, so it means we're accessing via the production network typically. Access is provided over common protocols, Telnet or SSH. And if we have an opportunity or a choice between Telnet and SSH, we should always choose SSH. Telnet is not encrypted, so therefore not secure, whereas SSH is an encrypted connection. Also with in-band, we're closer to the point of entry into the network, typically. Also less to manage and reconfigure when inserting into the network. We don't have to do a lot of rerouting or trying to move traffic around to access those devices out-of-band. Conversely, out-of-band, more reactive in nature versus real time, so we're not monitoring that traffic in real time. It has to go up to some external or

out-of-band management device or some type of analytic device to monitor that traffic - not in real time. It also requires additional design or redesign to enter into or insert into the network and requires additional upstream provider components to provide similar security. The in-band is going to be less intrusive, less to manage and less to reconfigure. You get the idea. If we have the option between both, in-band's going to be less work; however, if the primary network goes down, our access goes down. So out-of-band gives us another way to access those devices. If we can't access the device via our primary or production network, we still have that access out-of-band, which gives us remote functionality. We don't have to drive to the data center or drive to wherever that location or that device is located, saving us time and effort. Then the last on our list is that endpoint compliance is not as granular, meaning client traffic is sent to a common VLAN. As an example, when clients enter our network and they want to be quarantined or checked for compliance, they're going to be sent to a common VLAN versus monitored in quarantine real time and separated from other clients entering the network. For a little more detail on in-band access control, here we have a client that is accessing an access switch. That access switch contains such things as a Policy Enforcement Point, or a PEP, an authenticator, and a Policy Decision

Point. This is for granted access, network access control, to our local area network. When we're doing in-band, that functionality is typically incorporated into the switch or some other device that's placed inline on our production network. To access the switch to go through this decision making process, the Policy Enforcement Point, the authenticator, and the Decision Point, it decides, does that client meet our specifications? Are they allowed to access the LAN? If that were an out-of-band process, then it would have to go out to some external device outside of our typical network, traffic would have to be rerouted, a client may get a different IP address while they're being authenticated, and then rerouted back onto the corporate LAN once they're authenticated. It adds some additional overhead and some architectural designs, just something to keep in mind. It's in our best interest if we had the opportunity to have both in-band and out-of-band management and access. If for some reason our primary network or our production network goes down, we still have access to those devices. Another example of out-of-band access will be an out-of-band NIC, so a separate interface for management networks, whether that is a management VLAN or a separate physical network. It's used for lights out management. That way, we can monitor and audit or log. We can also use the patch, install operating systems or troubleshoot a host that is offline and won't boot. Typically, we can remote into a desktop or a server using RDP or some type of remote connection software. But if that actual device won't boot or is not operational, and therefore the remote desktop software or the remote control software is not functioning, we're dead in the water. If we have an out-of-band NIC that has a lights out functionality or lights out feature, we can still access as if we're sitting at that PC or at that server. That gives us the opportunity to manage, patch, reboot, even when the server at the OS level is down. It saves us a trip to the data center.

Port Security and 802.1x

The next concept I want to talk about is about port security in 802.1x - securing physical access to the network. What do I mean by that? Well, we want to control the ability of someone to just walk into our environment, whether it be at a kiosk or retail store or a library or a school, or even within our corporate environment, we don't want necessarily someone to be able to walk up, pull out their laptop, pull out a Cat 5 cable, plug it into the wall and get access to our network. One way we can do that is through something called port security. This is particularly applicable to things like kiosks, and schools, and libraries, but not necessarily throughout an entire environment as it becomes a little bit unwieldy at that point, but for specialized situations that we want to control specific access to specific ports, port security is definitely a good fit. What we can do is configure a switch so that it only learns one MAC address per port We can keep attackers from sending multiple fake addresses, someone can't pull out their laptop, plug in and then just start bombarding our network with fake MAC addresses, because, if you recall, when we have our devices and it connects to a switch, that very first time it does, it goes out and tries to get an IP address via DHCP, or it may have one hard-coded. It's going to try also to ARP for some resources. It might go to DNS, it might go to whatever the case might be, trying to resolve a URL. Whatever action is taking place, it's going to put datagrams or data packets onto the network. As soon as it does that, the MAC address of that device is attached to that datagram, and then it gets recorded within that switch, whatever switchport it's connecting to. The switch, which is a Layer 2 device, will learn or memorize the MAC address and associate it with that port, and so the switch will learn over time all of the devices that are connected to it, what MAC addresses are associated with which ports, so that way when information comes in, it knows what port to send that information out of. It's a very directed process. Broadcasts will go out of all ports, but if there is traffic between PC 1 and PC 2, as an example, PC 1 is connected to Port 1, PC 2 is connected to, say, Port 10 in this example, it will only go in Port 1 and only out of Port 10, so that way it keeps things more secure. However, we have malicious individuals or malicious activity that can take place, where someone could flood a specific port and overrun the MAC table on that switch and bring it down. By setting port security and allowing only certain MAC addresses, or in this case one MAC address per port, we negate that ability for someone to do that type of activity. We can also use that in conjunction with something called 802.1x to strengthen security at the wall jack, with school settings as an example, or a kiosk. We have something called 802.1x authentication, which is EAPOL, or Extensible Authentication Access Protocol over LAN, or local area network. That Extensible Authentication Access Protocol gives us the ability to say, when somebody connects to our wall jack, we're not going to allow them to communicate until they authenticate with the network. In this example, they're going to authenticate with something referred to as a RADIUS server, it's an authentication server. In this schema it's a multi-part process. The client in this case is referred to as a supplicant. The client is going to initiate a request, they're going to plug into a wall jack, let's say, as an example, they take out their laptop, and they plug it into the jack. They're going to say, can I communicate, can I get an IP address. The switch is going to say, no way, not until you authenticate. It will only allow EAPOL traffic to pass through that port. It will send it off to the authentication server, all of these things have to be configured in place so that this process takes place properly, but once it's set up, that port will not be activated until the authentication process is complete. The supplicant will send information over to the switch. The switch will then forward it on to the authentication server. Once that authentication server validates, once the credentials are validated and verified, in other words, the client is authenticated, the authentication server sends that information back and says, yes, you can communicate. The port is wide open, and of course the supplicant, or the client in this case, can communicate on the network.

Loop Protection and Flood Guards
When we're discussing ensuring availability on our network, another concept that you need to be familiar with is loop protection and flood guards. We talked about securing physical access to the network. We want to make sure that the network is available for someone to securely access. By ensuring availability via flood guards and loop protection, we have a couple concepts we need to talk about. Loop protection is a Layer 3 context.

Remember, Layer 3 deals with IP routing and with the network. It's the network layer of the OSI model, and routers live with this layer. Layer 3 deals with, routing IP packets across the network. As those IP packets travel, every time they cross over a router or every time they hop, they decrement with something called a TTL, or a Time to Live. Every time they cross over a router, that TTL will decrement by one. An IP packet, has a finite lifespan to live on the network. If it lives too long, then the packet gets dropped. In other words, if it doesn't reach its destination in a certain amount of time or a certain number of hops, it gets dropped. And that's specifically designed to prevent packets from just endlessly looping around the network. As an example, we have a couple networks separated by some routers, and in a normal fashion, the packet will just traverse those routers. Every time it crosses over, it decrements by one. The TTL will decrement. The routers know how to get from point A to point B. The packet goes from one network to the other. In a misconfigured situation, however, we have that packet, it would traverse the network, and it would just loop endlessly. If it were to do that and just loop forever, we would have a flood, and it would bring the network down. If the routers aren't configured properly, and they don't exactly know where to send the packet, router A thinks it should go here, router B thinks it should go somewhere else, it's going to get in a looping scenario. And if we didn't have that TTL in place, the Time to Live, every time it crosses over one of those routers it decrements, if that weren't in place, that packet would loop endlessly forever. And then as the next packet were to come onto the network, there'd be no room left. There'd be no bandwidth. As you can imagine, very quickly, that network would get overrun. By having that TTL in place, we negate that scenario from occurring.

Chapter 6 Spanning Tree, DHCP Snooping & MAC Filtering

In the layer 2 space, we don't have the TTL benefit. We don't have the ability to decrement. Layer 2 of the OSI model deals with things like switches and bridges. In layer 2, we have something referred to as a Spanning Tree Protocol, or STP. This accomplishes the same thing as a loop protection. It just does it in a different fashion. Spanning Tree Protocol is typically unable to prevent layer 2 loops, so switches can also prevent ports from flooding the network by clamping down once broadcasts hit a certain percentage. As an example, we have two switches. We have information that needs to pass from point A to point B. But if we have switches, which are multi-port bridges, and information comes in one port, goes out another, if the switch doesn't know exactly which port to send it out of, you can get in a looping situation. If switch A sent out Fa0/1 to switch B Fa0/1, and then switch B sent Fa02 out to switch A's Fa0/2, you can just see, we get in this looping fashion. What we have is the concept of an election. That election takes place between things called a root bridge, a designated bridge, and a root port. The root bridge is the center of the network. The designated bridges or the designated bridge are forwarders. They're going to send data to the root bridge, and then the root port is the port that sends data toward the root bridge. And if we didn't have the ability to shut down the non-necessary ports, we would just get loops all over the place. It doesn't mean those other paths aren't available. It just means they're not active. If we have a failover situation where that path becomes inactive or fails, the switches would then failover and activate those ports. It might take a few seconds, maybe 15 to 20 seconds potentially, depending upon the size of the network. But, a certain amount of time for all those things to synchronize and go through this process until all the other paths come up. But the network would, as you can imagine, it would heal itself. It gives us the ability to clamp down and not have these looping situations, but it doesn't take those other ports out of play. It just puts them in a non-active state. If it identifies that something needs to be brought up, maybe another port is down, it will bring those ports back up. It might take a little bit to converge so that everyone knows about the path so that all the switches know how the network is laid out. But once those ports come back up, the network will heal itself. At any one point in time, we only want one path from point A to point B., incidentally, root bridges are designated by the lowest MAC address, typically. As you can imagine, the lowest MAC address is going to be more than likely the oldest device on your network. You don't want to necessarily let the automatic process take place and allow that root bridge to be elected automatically because it's more than likely going to be the oldest device, and you might have, the least capability on that device. By manually selecting the root bridge, you can pick perhaps a more beefy switch or a newer piece of equipment so that we can ensure just a higher level of stability within the network.

DHCP Snooping

DHCP snooping sounds like that might be something an attacker or a bad actor might do, but DHCP snooping is a layer 2 security technology that monitors for rogue DHCP servers. What we're talking about is an actor will be on the opposite end of this specific technology. They would try to install or implement a DHCP server, a rogue DHCP server that hands out IP addresses, binding that MAC address to an IP address and giving them the ability to potentially compromise that system. Switches can be configured to prevent malicious or malformed DHCP packets. You can in essence turn that on so that if it detects malformed packets or malicious packets or it's coming from a server that's not a trusted or already configured or preconfigured DHCP server, then it would drop that packet. When a violation is detected, the event will be logged and alerts should be generated for further follow up or action, security personnel should be alerted and they should follow that up to see hey, what's going on on the network? Why is there a rogue DHCP server? Why is there someone that we don't know about trying to hand out DHCP packets?

MAC Filtering

MAC filtering, or Media Access Control filtering predefines which Media Access Control addresses can connect to a router or an access point. MAC addresses reside at layer 2 of the OSI model, and it's a 48-bit hex number that's burned into the NIC, or the network interface card. That won't prevent a skilled hacker from spoofing an allowed MAC address. A hacker with even a modest amount of skills and the toolsets can monitor or sniff the wire, understand what MAC addresses are valid, and then spoof the MAC address to allow themselves onto the network. With regard to MAC filtering, here we have a copy of Wireshark, and we're capturing packets on the network. From there, we can expand that out and dig down and see the MAC addresses of hosts communicating on the network. MAC addresses are very easy to spoof. Tools like Kali Linux, which we talked about briefly, and Wireshark can allow an attacker to scan a network and discover valid MAC addresses. Using things like aireplay-ng or aircrack-ng, we can send what's called deassociation packets to the client and then connect in that clients place. These tools exist. It's not something that you have to be particularly skilled for. If you have the distribution of Linux, Kali Linux, in this case, a lot of these tools are already built in, or you can go out to the web and download these tools. These things can be done manually or even faster via scripts. It can take literally a matter of seconds to sniff the wire, grab a valid MAC address, send a deassociation packet, reconnect as that client, and then you're on the network. The takeaway being, don't develop that false sense of security and think, hey, I have MAC filtering in place. Only authorized clients can connect. Well, as we see, that's very easy to bypass. Always remember the mantra of defense in depth. We have to place multiple locks on the door so that if they are able to bypass one is to have another and then another and another to get through. Hopefully with enough locks on the door that we can make enough noise that we can hear them trying to come in or they'll say this is too difficult and then move on to somewhere else. In summary, we talked about load balancing, we talked about network segmentation, virtual private networks. We talked about DNS, along with network access control, or NAC. Also talked about out-of-band management and also port security.

Chapter 7 Access Control Lists & Route Security

In this chapter we'll start off with network appliances. We'll talk about access control lists, or ACLs, along with route security. We'll talk about quality of service along with implications of IPv6, port spanning and port mirroring, along with port taps. We'll also talk about monitoring services and then file integrity monitors. First, let's talk about the concept of a jump server. A jump server is a server that's used to connect to devices in remote networks, typically used to perform admin tasks in a network with limited connectivity. What do I mean by that? Well, there might be issues with firewalls, with bandwidth, you may have a remote office or an area of your existing network, or your local network that you can't get to very easily. You may have firewalls in place that will block a lot of the tools that you may need to do work in that subnet, but normally, you can remote into a server, you can open up the ports to allow remote connectivity, an RDP session, or a Citrix session, or open up some type of VDI desktop, in that specific subnet, and then you can do all your things local in that subnet. So, the only thing it's passing through the firewall is your remote connectivity traffic. Everything else is taking place as if you were sitting in that subnet. The jump server allows you to perform those tasks without having to worry about punching holes in the firewall, and then additionally, from an admin's perspective, a lot of times when you have like vendors come in, or you're doing some type of work, patching or upgrading, you don't want to necessarily tie up the admin's workstation or laptop doing those remote tasks, especially when it comes to maintenance work or patching. By utilizing a jump server, you can have a vendor or someone you're working with also remote into that server, and they can work off that local server rather than the admin's workstation, or the admin's laptop. It serves a dual purpose and allows connectivity, but it also allows you to perform tasks without tying up your workstation. Some security risks will exist potentially if it's not configured and maintained, if it's bridging networks? If you have a jump server that's sitting between two networks, which is typically not good, a dual-homed machine, typically that's going to be a no-no, but if the jump server is maintained correctly, if it's patched properly, if it's maintained just like any other server on your network, then you should be in pretty good shape, but just understand that security risks do exist. If it's a remote office, and it's something that you forget about, and you don't patch, and you don't maintain regularly, well, that's going to pose potentially a security risk, so keep those things in mind.

Proxies

Let's talk about proxies and the difference between a forward and a reverse proxy. As far as forward proxies are concerned, which is what we're typically used to, a forward proxy normally have a number of clients that are trying to access some type of internet resource. What they're going to do is forward the requests to the proxy. The proxy then goes to the internet out to the external resources. What it does is potentially speed up access or the appearance of speeding up access for clients internal to the network and everyone attaching to the proxy. If someone else is already contacted that resource previously and that content has not yet expired on the proxy, well then the client will retrieve most if not all of that information from the proxy rather than going out to the actual resource. Some content is dynamic. Some things need to be refreshed constantly. Not everything will be retrieved from the proxy potentially. Again, it depends upon the resource being accessed. But it does a few things. It speeds up or potentially speeds up the access, but it can also act as a network address translation or a NAT device and hide the actual IP addresses or the internal IP addresses of the clients inside the network from external resources. So from any one of the websites that they see on the web servers, what they see is a request coming from the proxy server. They never see the actual internal clients requesting that access. They'll see the public-facing IP address of the proxy server, but not the internal IP addresses of the resources on that internal network. Conversely, there's something referred to as a reverse proxy, otherwise known sometimes as a load balancer. We have external resources, clients from the outside, wanting to connect to some internal resource, whether that be a web server or a database server. We have all the external clients coming in from the internet. We're going to hit the reverse proxy or load balancer. This could be one server. It could be a pool of servers. What it does is then take that request and then forward it on to the appropriate resource. It could be four servers. It could be 40. It could be 400. It just depends upon the size of the network and the resources. The reverse proxy or the load balancer will then take those incoming requests and distribute that request onto the available resources, and it will do so in a very programmatic fashion. Some load balancers or reverse proxies are more advanced than others. Some do it in more of a round-robin fashion where it just distributes the load across one server, then the next, then the next. Others have advanced algorithms where they'll be able to tell dynamically which server is least busy and will forward the request to that resource. Next, we have something referred to as a transparent proxy. A transparent proxy is an intermediary system that typically sits between a user and a content provider. It can be multi-purpose as well. It can do caching. It can do filtering, which is content filtering or application filtering, websites or services. It can allow or deny based upon type of content or a specific type of website or a service. And it can also provide gateway functionality, which is rule based, typically requiring registration or user acceptance. A lot of times in public spaces, coffee shops, you'll see these captive portals, that are, in effect, a gateway, a transparent proxy, that requires a user to register in some fashion, maybe a username, or at least accept some type of end user agreement to provide access. The transparent proxy gets its name from the fact that an end user doesn't have to configure anything. Typically, with a proxy, a user will configure something within their browse or to point to a proxy server. With a transparent proxy, there is no configuration needed. As soon as that user attaches to the network, whether it be Wi-Fi, the requests are automatically intercepted by that transparent proxy, and then some type of application filtering or content filtering is applied, or the user's prompted to register or accept some type of end user agreement before they access the network.

Web Security Gateways

Security gateways or a proxy server with advanced features, such things as virus scanning, it could prevent connections to inappropriate sites like peer-to-peer networks or file sharing sites, data loss prevention, which is a big thing nowdays, so if it determines or it can sense, does this communication contain nine digits maybe with two dashes, maybe a social security number, or does it contain 16 digits for a credit card number or, so it can identify different types of traffic and block that from escaping the network. Or you can block connections to inappropriate sites, peer-to-peer, file sharing, dropbox, box.net. A lot of users, even in the corporate environment, will use these types of services like Dropbox to share files back and forth, primarily because it's easy, but the downside of that is, there is no governance around that? A lot of companies want to restrict access to those types of sites so they can much more tightly control what types of data is leaving their network. You can also block things like ActiveX controls, Java applets, third-party cookies, malicious websites have a lot less chance of infecting or doing damage in a corporate environment if those attack vectors are mitigated. Activex control, Java applets, a lot of times malware or misbehaving sites utilize or leverage those specific technologies to inflict harm on users. It can also enable granular access to websites so that you can access the website, but maybe not all of the website? In other words, you could access LinkedIn, for instance, but not allow someone to do a job search or you could allow people to access Facebook, but prohibit them from posting content or playing games.

Chapter 8 Intrusion Detection and Prevention

The next thing is going to be intrusion detection and prevention. This is another security concept. We have an IDS and an IPS, NIDS and NIPS. Network intrusion detection system or prevention systems vary a little bit in how they operate. There is a lot of commonality, but then as far as the lack of action that they take, this differentiates the two. They can be used to log alert or take action when suspicious activity occurs on the network. Depending upon how they are configured, they can either simply detect that there is activity taking place and I'll go ahead and log it, or they could take action and say, as soon as this happens, do A, B, and C. They may reset a TCP connection, they may block a port, they may kick off some type of a forensic data capturing activity We have active systems that can take action to prevent an attack, or we have passive systems that simply record and perhaps utilize that data for later analysis. In terms of the difference between IDS and IPS, the network part aside, just generally speaking, we have intrusion detection systems and intrusion prevention systems. IDS has been around for quite a while, fairly common, and it's easy or relatively easy to set up, but as you may gather from what we've talked about already, it simply logs, alerts, and events, so it detects the intrusion, it doesn't necessarily do anything with it, it may alert an administrator or something, but it's not going to kick off any preventative measures. So it allows for a reactive response and further research into malicious or suspicious activity. An IPS, or an intrusion prevention system, is a newer platform, it's been around for the last few years, but it enables prevention. Such as perhaps blocking an IP address, blocking a port, resetting TCP connections, their TCP/IP connections, those types of things. It takes some type of preventive measure to shut down that communication or shut down that action so that malicious activity is halted in its tracks. The downside with an intrusion prevention system is you could have a false positive that could ultimately block legitimate traffic. Worst case scenario, let's just say, for example, you have an IPS set up, and if it detects malicious activity, go ahead and block port 80 for 5 minutes. Well, you could have legitimate traffic that comes in, maybe just a heavier than normal workload that comes in that IPS would falsely identify that as malicious traffic when it's not, shuts down the internet traffic over port 80 shuts that down for 5 minutes, well, you've just created a Denial of Service against yourself. Those things have to be set up with care, as that they do have the potential for false positives, but it also gives you the ability to prevent things, when in fact, you do have malicious activity taking place. The different components of intrusion prevention and detection systems; I'm going to go through a list but this is more just for your informational purposes than anything, but we have a couple components that you need to be aware of. We have alerts. an alert is a message generated from something called an analyzer and the analyzer indicates anything that it may deem as interesting traffic or an interesting event has occurred, so that alert might be an email, that alert might be a pop up on a screen. In some form or fashion, it's going to alert us that something has occurred. The analyzer processes data collected from one or more sensors. The sensor collects data or triggers data and then it looks for suspicious activity and the analyzer is going to take that data and look for what it deems to be suspicious or malicious activity, it could be deterministic, or it could be rule-based. We could just say, hey, if it meets this signature, than it's probably malicious, go ahead and fire off some type of alert or some type of action. The data source itself is the raw data that's being analyzed. That could be log files, it could be audit logs, system logs, network traffic itself, it just depends. It depends on the system and it depends upon how it's configured. Then we have something called an event. An event is an indication, that something suspicious has occurred, it could be malicious, it could be suspicious, it could be a false positive, but in some fashion, the system has determined that this needs further investigation, so that can trigger an alert or notification. Or if it's confirmed and it is malicious activity, then that event would become an incident. Next we have a component called a manager, and the manager is the intrusion detection system console, that's the piece of software that comes up on your screen and that's what you use to manage the system. Next is a notification, which is the process by which the operator, which is someone who is working the system here, they are alerted to an event or an incident. The operator, as I said as a user, it could be an admin, someone that's responsible for that intrusion detection system. They're actively working the system. They don't necessarily need to be sitting there. They could be alerted remotely, email, but there is someone that's responsible for the operation of that system. And then the sensor is a primary data collection point for that intrusion detection system, or the IDS. A sensor could be a device driver, it could be baked into a piece of firmware on a system, or it could be a separate physical device that's attached to a network that collects data, so it could be a separate device collecting data and then processing that in real time.

IDS/IPS Component Workflow

If we look at the components of an IDS system and how they all fit together, it may make a little more sense. We have a data source, we have a couple sensors, we have the analyzer, the active response and then a manager, and then the administrator and the operator. There are security policies that will tie all of this together. The security policies dictate what action is taken. The administrator and the operator may also analyze some of this data for trending and reporting purposes. And an active response could trigger some type of action, whether it be shutting down a port or whether it be resetting connections. The data source has some type of activity, the sensors will pick up on that, and it will generate an event. That event goes to the analyzer to be analyzed, is this something that I need to be worrying about, and if it is, it generates an alert to the manager or the management console. That console sends a notification to the operator or the administrator, depending upon, who's who, that can be used for trending or reporting purposes only. We just want to know about it, we're not going to do anything at this point. Or it could send off an active response and say, wait a minute, we need to do something here, that's when it triggers the shutting down of a port or resetting of a connection.

Four Approaches to IDS

There are four approaches that I want you to know about as far as IDS systems are concerned. We have behavior-based detection. That's variations of behavior, increased traffic, policy violations, something that's just out of the norm. We have signature-based IDS systems, and that's going to use attack signatures and audit trails. In other words, look for traffic that looks like it might be IP spoofing or might be cross-site injection, or it might be somebody hammering, doing a port scan on our external firewalls. It could be a thousand different things, but there are going to be signatures that it's going to be looking for. They're not necessarily as robust has some of the other systems because if the signature doesn't exist or if it's a brand new, let's say, for instance, a zero-day exploit or a zero-day threat, meaning there is no signature defined yet, then those things are vulnerable to be bypassed. We have anomaly detection IDS systems, and, again, similar to behavior based in that it learns what's normal, then it looks for deviations from that baseline. In this instance, over time it's going to learn, 30% workload is normal for this specific segment. All of a sudden, if it's 60 or 70% above workload, all of a sudden we've got a ton of IP connections coming in, well, that's not normal. Go ahead and kick off some type of trigger or some type of an alert. It just depends upon what's normal for that specific environment. What's normal for one may not be normal for another. Then we have heuristic IDS, and that's going to utilize algorithms to analyze data traffic as it passes through. It's not signature based in that it has a certain set of parameters that it looks for. It has some type of internal algorithm that's going to depend upon the system so it will vary from place to place or from system to system, but it's going to use that algorithm to analyze the traffic as it passes through the system in real time and then make a determination at that point.

Network-based IDS
When you have network-based IDS systems, you can place those in a couple different places within the network. You can place them in front of your firewall, you could place them behind your firewall, or you could do both. For example, if I have an IDS system placed in front of the firewall. People from the internet are trying to get into my network, whether it's web servers or there's some type of a public-facing component that they can access. Rather than have them hit the firewall first, and then if they pass the muster, and they pass through the firewall, then if I hit the IDS system and I start analyzing traffic, well that's great, I have a reduction in the amount of stuff I have to analyze, but I don't get a good indication or a good idea of potentially

who's banging against the firewall, who's potentially trying to initiate some type of an attack. Conversely, if I do what I have here in the picture and I have the IDS system placed in front of the firewall, well, I'm going to get a lot more traffic to analyze, but I'm also going to get a better indication of attacks against that firewall. If you want to look at the best of both worlds, you would place an IDS system in front of your firewall and behind. That way you get a good indication of everything that's banging against the firewall. Some gets in, some doesn't. Once it passes through the firewall, then you have a secondary IDS system that can dig deeper and look for variations in policy or anomalies, depending upon the type of system. that's going to write out to some type of an event data database, and there's lots of different ones out there, and then typically, that's going to pass those types of things, once it has a trigger for an alert or notification, up to the network operations center, or a NOC, depending upon the size of the environment, you may or may not have a NOC in place, or you may use a third party for that purpose. But then the NOC is going to either take some type of remediation immediately, they may have some steps, they have some NOC analysts that will say, hey, if this happens, do ABC. Or they may page out a person who's on call, if it's after hours, or engage a specific team to come in and take some action. It simply just depends upon the size of the company.

Security Device Placement

When we're talking about security device placement, we have things like sensors, collectors, correlation engines, filters, proxies, firewalls, VPN concentrators, SSL accelerators, distributed denial-of-service mitigators, aggregation switches, and taps and port mirrors. I'm just calling all of these things out you're aware of what they are and understand that any of these things, for the most part, can be placed in various places within the network. They could be placed internally. They could be placed on the perimeter. They could be placed in a DMZ on a firewall in either location or in multiple locations. In the case of sensors, as an example, you may have sensors all throughout the network on many devices, both internal and external, and they may all feedback to your intrusion detection or prevention system to let you know if somebody is trying to get into the network in some fashion or people are logging in when they're not supposed to, doing something that they're not authorized to do so. Collectors are along the same lines. Sensors and collectors, correlation engines, they all take that information and they correlate across multiple devices to show you a common timeline to help identify trends. Filters, proxies and firewalls, are typically going to go on the perimeters. They will filter content, they'll filter access requests. Proxies, as we know, will aggregate requests internally. And then that way, the person requesting a website or some resource internally if someone else just recently requested the same thing doesn't have to go out to the internet to that device. I can pull it from the proxy. Firewalls, we know what a firewall does. It blocks based on port or protocol or some type of application and only allows things through that we want to allow through. VPN concentrators, we talked about. SSL accelerators or load balancers can again be placed in front of say a web server, could be placed in front of an application server, and they can be spun up dynamically if we're using something like SDN so that we can add additional resources when we need them. Same thing with DDoS mitigators - it can detect automatically when we're having a denial-of-service attack and it can shut down ports or take some type of response to mitigate that threat. Aggregation switches will aggregate data from smaller switches, you'll have a small network and an aggregation switch that will combine a number of small networks. They could be placed anywhere throughout the network, depending upon how your network is architected, whether it's a mesh, a full mesh, a core edge. Then we have taps and port mirrors. And what it does is place that switch or that port in what's called promiscuous mode. That way you can mirror the traffic on another port, and typically that's done from mirroring or auditing or forensic investigations you can mirror all the traffic on a specific port and then analyze that without affecting the traffic on the port itself.

Chapter 9 Firewalls & Unified Threat Management

What's the actual purpose of firewalls? Well, a firewall is, generally speaking, designed to isolate one network from another. It can be hardware or it can be software based. It can be either. It can be a standalone device, or it can be an integrated device integrated into some other equipment, in other words, routers or switches. Whether you're a small office or a home office, you may have a small Netgear or Linksys or even a Cisco router, that combines a lot of functionality together. You can have a firewall. It can do NAT, or Network Address Translation, and, of course, routing functionality as well, perhaps even switching. It just depends on the size of the network, how specific you want to get. There are different devices that can perform very specific functions, or there are integrated devices that can perform a lot of different functions together. If we have a diagram of outside users outside of the firewall, and you see the firewall denoted by a brick wall. And, incidentally, the term firewall historically came from buildings that were built very close to one another, and in order to prevent fire from jumping from one building to another when they were very close together, think like row homes, for instance, they would build these brick walls in between these different buildings to prevent that fire from jumping from one to the other. That brick wall would act as a firewall, to prevent fire from jumping from one building to the other. The same concept is carried over here. And that's why you typically see a firewall being illustrated as a brick wall. As you can then imagine, firewalls are typically used to block or limit outside traffic from entering a network. Whether it's corporate, medium-sized office, small office, or a home office, they all serve pretty much the same types of functions. However, firewalls can also be placed internally, inside of a network to segment one area from another. For instance, you may have a large corporate environment that has different areas that you don't necessarily want them to communicate, or they shouldn't communicate, from one to the other very easily. You can punch holes in the firewall to allowed traffic. But, generally speaking, these things are cordoned off from one another. For instance, if you have a PCI Secure zone, like say you have a very large enterprise that has some typical day-to-day workers, and you may have an R&D department, you may have an accounting department, a finance department, PCI Secure means it contains credit card information and some type of personally identifiable information. You want to have that information cordoned off from the rest of the network. The finance folks don't necessarily talk to the R&D or maybe the graphics department, just to prevent internal browsing of those resources. A firewall can be put into place between those segments on your internal network as well. It's important to understand, and just to recap very quickly hardware vs. software, firewalls can either be hardware or software based. They can be standalone devices or integrated into other devices, like routers and switches. Even if it is a hardware-based solution, it's still going to contain software, you can't just run it on hardware by itself. There has to be some software running behind the scenes. You can drop it onto a server and have that server function providing firewall functionality. Or it can be a separate, standalone piece of hardware. However, that hardware is still going to contain software or firmware. What are some types of firewalls? Well, we have packet filtering firewalls, and packet filtering firewalls allow or block traffic based upon a specific port, HTTP traffic as an example, web traffic that typically comes in over port 80. FTP, or File Transport Protocol, that's generated on port 21 typically. You can configure the firewall to allow web traffic but don't allow FTP traffic or allow DNS but don't allow NetBIOS or time lookups or whatever the case might be. You can break it down by port by port by port and get very specific, get very granular. Doing it based just on port, there's not a lot of intelligence there. It just simply looks at the port, and then it will either allow or block the traffic at that point. Next, we have proxy firewalls. a proxy firewall is going to be dual homed, which means it's going to have two network interfaces, typically one on each network or on separate networks. It's going to segment internal users from the outside world, and it can mask the IP address using something called NAT, or Network Address Translation. That gives an added layer of security because the outside world won't know who is communicating. All they'll see is the address of the proxy firewall. And a proxy can also cache requests to improve perceived speed. If you have multiple users as an example that are accessing the same website, well, the first person to access that website or that URL will go out and pull it down from the web or from whatever resource it's getting it from. Subsequent requests, as long as that information is still sitting in the cache on that proxy server, so the next user goes out to that same web resource? Instead of going out to the web out to whatever resource they're getting it from, they'll get it directly from the proxy server, from the cache. It gives the perception that things are faster and that your network is all of a sudden more responsive. The next type of firewall is something referred to as a stateful packet inspection firewall, or SPI. An SPI firewall examines the packets and keeps the packet table of every communication channel. So, in other words, it has more intelligence than a simple packet filtering firewall, and it does a deeper dive, examines what's inside. SPI tracks the entire conversation, so it gives you an increased level of security because it only allows packets from known active connections. In other words, if someone's trying to spoof or jump into the middle of a connection or a conversation, an SPI firewall understands that. They say, hey, wait a minute. I don't know who this is from. I haven't seen this before. This is in the middle of a conversation. There's no initiation. There's no back and forth to establish that connection. This just came out of here, so I'm going to drop that. It drops the packet. It gives you that added layer of security. It's better than simple packet filtering, which only looks at the current packet. However, it's possible to attack by overloading that State Table. As you go through all of these different types of routers and switches and pretty much any type of infrastructure or equipment in our network, just understand that nothing is foolproof. There's always going to be a way, there are always going to be hackers that are trying to somehow penetrate that device, crash it, and get elevated privileges. Nothing's foolproof. That's while we're all employed and how we all eventually make the big bucks. The battle goes on and on and on. Check Point Software introduced the concept of a stateful inspection or stateful packet inspection firewall in the use of its FireWall-1 software, which was introduced in 1994. So, it's been around for quite a while.

Web Application Firewalls

A web application firewall differs from a network firewall in that it operates at the application layer of the OSI model. Web application firewalls, or WAF, operates at application layer 7 of the OSI model. That's, the application layer, and it's designed with very specific or granular rules for web servers. And these types of firewalls can analyze traffic to prevent typical web server type attacks, such as, SQL injection attacks, cross-site scripting attacks or forged HTTP requests. Any time you see a website that has a form that you can fill in, very skilled hackers, can craft either a cross-site scripting or SQL injection attacks, and they'll write SQL code that they'll use as the code in the form. It may ask you for your name, as an example, on a web form. Well, instead of putting in your name, the hacker will try to put in some type of long SQL code, some SQL query, and if it's formed correctly, it can crash that server. If the server's not protected against that, if it doesn't sanitize that input properly, then it can initiate some type of SQL query on the back end and perhaps crash that web server or crash the website, return some type of information, or even give some type of increased elevated privileges to the server. That's why these types of firewalls are in place, to understand these things as they come in in real time, analyze what's happening, and shut it down before it has a chance to do any harm., some well-known web application firewall vendors, just for your own knowledge, are things like Cisco, Citrix, Barracuda Networks, F5, and eEye. There are probably 30 or 40 more well-known vendors, but these are just a few to give you an example. If you wanted to dig a little bit further, these are just some of the major players in that space. As an example of a firewall, there's one from Check Point and they run the gamut from small firewall appliances, and it gets bigger and bigger as we go on. We have an entire chassis system with blades installed. They can range from very small software-based implementations, to small hardware-based implementations, and on up. Depending upon the size of the company and the enterprise, they can go from a few hundred dollars up to tens of thousands of dollars and more.

Unified Threat Management (UTM)
We've talked about VPNs, and firewalls, and intrusion detection and prevention systems, and all of these different things as individual pieces of software or individual applications, but there's also something referred to as a UTM, or Unified Threat Management suite. That's a multipurpose suite of tools, and it does things such as firewalls, network

intrusion detection or prevention systems, gateway anti-virus and anti-spam. It can provide VPN functionality, content filtering, load balancing, and also DLP or data loss prevention. These newer types of tools can pretty much do everything and take the place of all of these individual components. The advantage being you have a single pane of glass that you can look at all of these things, and you can correlate events across all these different applications much easier as well. It makes troubleshooting and also incident or event investigation much easier. If you haven't taken a look at these yet, I highly recommend that you look at some of the UTM software that's available and see if it fits within your environment. It could save you some time and effort in deployment, troubleshooting, patching, and also incident or event management.

Content Filters

A content filter can be hardware or software, and its purpose is to limit or restrict access to certain types of content. Inappropriate material, it could be malware, viruses, could be worms or trojans, and also things like spam or spyware. Misconfigured devices can overblock or allow content that should, in fact, be filtered. Additionally, these things can also violate censorship laws and regulations, depending upon your location or what you're filtering. Content filters are, in fact, valid. I'm not saying they shouldn't be there, just that an extra level of due diligence should be placed on them to make sure that they're configured properly, that they're blocking what they should be blocking, We don't develop that false sense of security. Something else to keep in mind is that these things can be built into firewalls, UTM devices, or they could be standalone software. They don't necessarily have to be a specific separate device. They can be built into things like firewalls and Unified Threat Management, or UTM, devices.

Implicit Deny and ACLs

It's a firewall access control list, or an ACL, and it specifies what type of traffic is allowed. If it's not on the list, it denied access. Much like if you go into a club, or a restaurant, or some VIP event, and you walk up to the front door and the bouncer standing there all intimidating and you read off your name and say, hi, I'm so and so and he looks on his list and says, nope, you're not on the list. You're not getting in. Well, as frustrating as that might be, that's the same concept here. You walk up and your name is on the list, yeah, good for you. You can go in the front door, but if you're not explicitly allowed, then you're implicitly denied.

Route Security

Routers connect networks together and external routing protocols like BGP, or border gateway protocol, are inherently insecure. They were created years ago back when security wasn't a major concern. The main emphasis, at that point, was connectivity and getting everyone connected together, security and all the different types of threats that we face today weren't top of mind or even a consideration back then. What I'm talking about here with BGP specifically, it consists of autonomous systems, or AS groups, groups of systems that are managed by the same administrative system, Misconfigurations and deliberate route hijacks can result in outages. It's possible for someone to misconfigure their system and advertise routes that shouldn't be there and create outages. Typically, it's not necessarily a direct attack, although it can be, but oftentimes the outages that have been experienced in the past have been a result of misconfiguration on the systems. It's beyond the scope of this book to dig deeply into this, but I do want to call your attention to the NIST publication, NIST SP1800-14, which proposes securing BGP and they talk about things like route origin, validation, and also resource public key infrastructure, or RPKI. What it does in a nutshell is put some security guardrails, on the BGP protocol and only allow secure or preauthorized systems to communicate with each other and not allow rogue systems or misconfigured systems to advertise out on the internet so we can prevent some of the things that we've seen in the past. Unfortunately, this has not been widely adopted yet, but the proposal is out there, so I would encourage you to read more deeply if you want some more information on that specific topic.

Quality of Service (QoS)
QoS, or quality of service is a set of technologies to ensure critical applications or services have a certain level of performance. We're talking about packets that are marked to identify service types. You may have audio, video. You may have critical applications like in a medical facility or finance applications or things that just need a guaranteed level of bandwidth. It will reserve bandwidth for those applications, and then everyone else gets what's left. So routers prioritize packets, and they'll create virtual queues to ensure bandwidth. They put the most important applications to the front of the line. You can almost think of it like as a fast pass, if you would. If you've ever been to Disney World or some of these amusement parks, you have the concept of a fast pass you don't have to wait in the line or wait in the queue. This is a very similar type of scenario where we will mark the packets that we want to push to the front of the line. The

things we're talking about with quality of service, things like bandwidth and latency, the amount of bandwidth or how big is the pipe that they can go through. Latency being how much delay is there. Packet loss usually resolving around the fact that the network is too congested and the packets time out, so we lose those packets. Then something referred to as jitter, which refers typically to audio and video, where we have packets that arrive out of sequence or out of order, and it can make audio calls sound scrambled or digitized or it can create skipping in streaming applications. By ensuring quality of service, we make sure those applications that need that level of performance get what they need. Then as more and more IoT devices, or Internet of Things devices, come online, having bandwidth for real-time monitoring, as an example, becomes more and more important. Things that need real-time performance, real-time monitoring, so we need to make quick action or quick decisions based upon that information, QoS comes in handy because it allows us to guarantee a certain level of performance for those applications and for those devices.

Implications of IPv6

Now let's talk about the implications of IPv6, or Internet Protocol version 6. So, IPv4 addresses, which have been around since the dawn of the internet, the mid-60s, late-60s, IP version 4 is a 32-bit addressing scheme. With that, roughly 4 billion IP addresses when it first came out, we thought, that's going to be more than we'll ever need, not a big deal. Well, as it turns out, as more and more devices have come online, we're running out of IP addresses. So, NAT, or network address translation helps to a degree. We could put a bunch of internal IPs behind one external IP. But as new devices come online, IoT devices, that problem will only continue to expand. And in some parts of the world, we've already run out of IPv4 addresses. IPv6 is natively enabled on most devices nowadays, so the issue is, the implication is, it's often overlooked and can mean open door if it's not secured properly. Sometimes if it's not configured properly, if it's not something you think about, you may say, well, I have IPv4 rules in place, I have things locked down, I'm good. But if IPv6 is enabled on the devices and it's not secured, it's just as is out of the box, well, that could have some security implications potentially. Security policies often aren't uniformly applied, from IPv4 to IPv6. Meaning the things that we have locked down with version 4, we don't necessarily have the same level of parity, or the same level of lockdown, when it comes to v6. That false sense of security in the IPv4 is locked down, it's filtered, but again, IPv6 could be wide open to attack. Another thing is with IPv6 being relatively new, although it's been around for a while, it's relatively new as far as actual adoption is concerned, that lack of experience with countermeasures against IPv6 hacks and attacks, so subject matter expertise is not as widespread, and hacking tools are taking advantage of IPv6 vulnerabilities. It's becoming more and more of a problem if we don't start to lock down these devices and make sure that things are turned off if we don't need it, or if we are using it, that it's secured properly. Hackers are taking advantage of this because the majority of the hacking tools that are out there are being upgraded, they're being patched, and, new versions coming out, just like regular traditional software or commercial software, they're upgrading their stuff as well. As new technologies come online, those tools are updated as well to take advantage of vulnerabilities in that new technology.

Port Mirroring, Port Spanning, and Port Taps
Now let's talk about the concept of port mirroring, so also known as port spanning or SPAN, or Switched Port Analyzer. What it does is a switch sends a copy of all network packets seen on a port, or it could be an entire VLAN, to another port to be analyzed. In other words, if you recall how a switch works, where it maintains a MAC table, a MAC table or MAC addresses of all the hosts attached to that

switch, and it knows what hosts live on what port. It only sends traffic out of the port that that host is connected to, so it helps to reduce traffic. When we're doing port spanning or a Switched Port Analyzer, we can copy all of the data off of a port, or the entire switch or an entire VLAN, and send that to another port and it can be analyzed, so intrusion detection systems, trouble shooting, we could use it for forensics, we could use it for user monitoring. Those things are in play to allow us to identify and monitor or dig into the packets on a specific port or a specific VLAN. As an example, if we have a switch, there are four ports on the switch, and then we have four computers attached to that switch. This is a traditional connectivity scenario. We have all of these different devices connecting to a switch. When we're talking about port mirroring, well, we have the same devices. Let's say, in this case we have three devices connected, and they're connected to that device via ports 1, 2, and 3, well, then we're also going to have a monitoring device on port 4, and that will utilize port mirroring. In the first scenario, the computer attached to port 1 wants to communicate with the computer on port 3. Well, since the MAC table exists on that switch, it knows where those two hosts live, and it only sends traffic out of the port that that host lives on, so that way it's reducing traffic and it helps make things more secure. But in the second scenario, you'll notice that all the PCs, or all the hosts connected to the switch, like they're communicating, well, all of that traffic gets sent out of port 4 to the port mirroring device, and it allows that port mirroring device to capture those packets, analyze those packets, and do whatever it needs to with that information. A similar concept would be port taps. In this instance we have East/West traffic, we talked about that before, traffic occurring inside the data center. All of the devices attached to the switch, if it needs to communicate to another network within our data center, it would send that to the router and then off to its destination. Well, a similar concept to port mirroring is something referred to as a port tap. In this situation we would insert a tap inline between those two devices, and that tap would then go out to out-of-band security or monitoring tools, so it would be placed inline and then capture all the packets and do it in real time. It's quicker and it's more efficient than doing port mirroring, where you don't have the potential of duplicating packets, doing it inline. However, it may or may not be applicable for your environment. This can work for Ethernet networks and then also Fibre Channel networks, but when we do these types of activities, they can be disruptive, so these things have to be planned out ahead of time to make sure that we don't disrupt connectivity between applications, between hosts and servers, but just two concepts to keep in mind that we can use to monitor traffic on a network.

File Integrity Check

A file integrity check protects against tampering by ensuring a file has not been modified. You can look at a few different things or a few pieces of metadata to understand if that file's been tampered with. You can look at credentials. You can look at privileges and security settings. You can also look at the content, the actual content of the file itself, attributes in size or hash values. If any of these things don't match, that's going to be indicative of some type of tampering, an indicator of compromise, perhaps the first steps in a larger breach. This might give you some advanced warning that someone's coming in, and they're starting to manipulate our files. We need to jump on this quickly, see if we can lock this down, perhaps follow what's going on, maybe even let that person do whatever it is they're doing for a short period of time while you monitor them you can then get a better understanding of who it is, where they're coming from. What happens is it's going to compare a current good state. It's going to take a baseline of that system, the file system, individual files. Typically it's going to run a hash against those files. If anything changes within that file, that hash value will be different. It's going to compare a current state against a known good state. If they don't match, then that's indicative of some type of compromise or tampering. As an example, Windows has something built in called the System File Checker, you can run that by running SFC. SFC will scan the integrity of all protected system files, and in this case it will replace ones that it finds either corrupt or changed or modified in some way with the correct Microsoft versions. You can do SCANNOW, VERIFYONLY. You can have it scan and then automatically repair what it finds, if it finds anything. Or you can say, go ahead and scan, but just verify only and report back to me. Don't repair anything yet. In the example down below, you have sfc /SCANNOW, or you can say VERIFYFILE, and you can point to a specific file You can check just one file at a time, not necessarily your entire file system. Or you can say, VERIFYONLY, and if you find anything, report back. That way you can take some further action if necessary. I summary we covered network appliances. We talked about access control lists, or ACLs. We talked about route security along with quality of service. We also covered the implications of IPv6, port spanning, port mirroring, and port taps, along with monitoring services and file integrity monitors.

Chapter 10 How to Install and Configure Wireless Security

In this chapter, we'll be talking about installing and configuring wireless security settings. We'll be talking about four main areas. We'll talk about cryptographic protocols, authentication protocols, also methods, and then installation considerations. Let's first cover some wireless definitions. WEP, or Wired Equivalency Protocol, was originally designed to provide security equal to a wired network. If you're familiar with WEP at you understand that it doesn't provide security at all anymore. It can be cracked within minutes or sometimes within seconds if you have the tools. Vulnerabilities have emerged, and this has since been deprecated. It's not recommended for a secure environment whatsoever. If you have no other choice and you have older legacy equipment in your environment that needs to communicate, in other words, make it backwards compatible, then you may have to have WEP. It's better than nothing, but not in the grand scheme of things. Anyone with an off-the-shelf-set of hacker tools or penetration testing tools, can crack WEP encryption relatively easily. The alternative to that, or the newer standards, would be Wi-Fi Protected Access, which is WPA or WPA2. WPA itself was based upon WEP, and it was used as a stop gap. WPA has also been cracked relatively quickly. WPA2, which is the newer standard, it fully implements 802.11i protocol, and that provides for additional security enhancements. We'll talk about why these things are so insecure, why we had some of these vulnerabilities to begin with. Then, for definitions sake, I want you to understand that Wireless Application Protocol, or WAP, not to be confused with wireless access point, which is also referred to with a WAP acronym, Wireless Application Protocol, that deals with mobile devices and providing mobile devices with internet connectivity. It's a suite of protocols similar to TCP/IP. But, it deals with mobile connectivity. It uses Wireless Transport Layer Security, or WTLS, similar to regular TLS that we would have seen in the TCP/IP suite when we're dealing with encryption or HTTPS, as TLS or SSL, as we spoke about in the previous chapter, and it provides for authentication, encryption, and data integrity.

WEP/WPA/WPA2

To define this a little bit further, with WEP, WPA, and WPA2, the standard WEP, used what was referred to as an RC4 stream, and it was a 24-bit encryption. The length of that encryption key is what led to its insecurity or its vulnerabilities. That IV, or the initialization vector, it's vulnerable to an IV attack, meaning that 24-bit encryption was not long enough. So, packet injection can crack WEP in literally several seconds. And what it boils down to is that initialization vector, 24-bits long is just too short. Every so often it has to repeat. There are only so many different combinations of initialization vectors that it can send. As communication takes place over any length of time, if someone's sitting there sniffing the wire for a period of time, they'll see that initialization vector. That's a hard one to say. They'll see that repeated every so often, so they'll be able to pull that off the wire because that IV, or the initialization vector, is static, and it's reused, and it's part of the RC4 encryption key. You already have a piece of the information once you understand what the initialization vector is, and it's also set in clear text. You have three or four pieces of the puzzle to begin with, and if you use standard penetration testing tools, those tools allow you to crack that encryption key very, very easily. It's not recommended for any type of secure environment. It should be avoided unless, backwards compatibility is needed.

WPA and WPA2 Security
As you move on to WPA and WPA2, WPA, or Wi-Fi-protected access that partially implements the 802.11i standard. It was a stopgap. It uses something called Temporal Key Integrity Protocol, or TKIP for Short and what it does is it takes a

128-bit wrapper, and it wraps that WEP encryption. That 24-bit encryption that we've already talked about as being too small, and it's reusable every so often, or it is reused every so often, it's too small. Well, with WPA, it wraps that entire encryption packet within 128-bit larger encryption packet. It generates a second key based upon the MAC address of the sender and the serial number of the packet. It mixes this key with the Initialization Vector, it mixes it with the IV, and it creates a per-packet key. It's more secure than WEP, but it's still using RC4 encryption, and it's backwards compatible with WEP. We know it is not considered a secure protocol because, again, it's been cracked very easily, again, using off-the-shelf tools. If we move to the next one, WPA2, that fully implements to 802.11i standard. That uses something called CCMP for enhanced security, or the CC-MAC protocol. It's Counter Mode Cipher Block Chaining Message Authentication Code Protocol. CCMP, it's 128-bit AES encryption algorithm. It's not backwards compatible with WEP, but it is much more secure. Having said that, is it completely secure? Is it completely foolproof? Well, the answer is No. That has also been cracked. Given enough time and if you have enough of a skilled hacker on the other end of sniffing that traffic, it is crackable. Wireless security examples. Well, WPA and WPA2 can use something called a Pre-shared Key, or PSK, or Enterprise Authentication. Pre-Shared Keys, if you have a home office or a small office home office, or a SoHo network, or a small business, you may be already familiar with Pre-Shared Keys. It means you have some password on the client. You have a password on your Wi-Fi router or your access point. As long as those two things match, then you can connect to the network. Enterprise uses something called RADIUS, which is an authentication server, and digital certificates. You have to have that certificate, and you have to have an account on that RADIUS server or some way to authenticate to that RADIUS server, so it provides for an even greater level of authentication. If we have a laptop that may again connect to a wireless access point. That wireless access point, if we're using Pre-Shared Key, all I need is that secret or that Pre-Shared Key on the laptop and on the wireless access point, and as long as they match, we connect and off we go. If we're using RADIUS, you'll see the laptop will connect to the wireless access point, or in a larger environment, you may have multiple wireless access points, in which case you would use a wireless LAN controller, and that way you can set up your information and your configuration once and push that out to all the wireless access points within your network. You can do that in one shot, so it just makes the management easier. But, you would connect to the wireless access point, which would forward your connection request over to the RADIUS server. The RADIUS server would check to see, is this person able to connect or authenticated to connect? Because if I can back up one, if we use a Pre-Shared Key, as long as we have the secret on both the laptop and the wireless access point, it connects. We don't know who it is that's connecting. If we're using authentication or Enterprise Authentication, then we have to authenticate with that RADIUS server. It's going to authenticate the user, as well as the laptop. This gives us a greater level of security.

WPA3
Before we get too much further along, let's talk about WPA3, which is the newest version of WPA and for all intents and purposes will replace WPA2. WPA2 is still very much in play, but WPA3 is making its way into the marketplace and into all the newer gear that's being released. WPA3 adds AES-GCMP, which is Galois/Counter Mode and also security jumps up from 128-bit SAE, and we'll talk about that in just a moment, to 192, which is optional for personal use. In actuality, it's 256-bit encryption, but the way things flush out when it's all said and done, it ends up being 192. SAE stands for Simultaneous Authentication of Equals, otherwise known as Dragonfly key exchange with forward secrecy feature, meaning If someone captures this

traffic and then tries to brute force it maybe six months, a year, and whatever down the road, they're not going to be able to do anything with it. That forward secrecy prevents brute force attacks and prevents someone from trying to decode that data at some future date. Key features, brute force protection. Also individualized encryption for each user using unauthenticated Diffie-Hellman Pairwise Master Key. In a nutshell, it's referred to as a PAKE, or a Password Authenticated Key Exchange. That provides mutual authentication and negotiates a fresh session key each time someone connects. That forward secrecy, is a prevention of offline dictionary attacks. If we look at this in more detail, it was released in 2018, and WPA3 is the successor to WPA2, and it offers several security enhancements. So 256-bit in actuality, but the overall effect for Wi-Fi is effectively 192-bit. Simultaneous Authentication of Equals, or SAE, You hear that term come up over and over again. Add that acronym with an abbreviation to your toolbag as well, also known as the Dragonfly key exchange with forward secrecy feature, as we've talked about. And then perhaps one of the biggest advancements is Opportunistic Wireless Encryption, or OWE, which protects unsecured networks such as libraries or coffee shops, airports or hotels. This will replace unencrypted open networks. So OWE will provide individualized data encryption to users connecting to public open networks to protect against eavesdropping. Each user gets their own distinct encrypted session without them having to do anything. On open networks, an attacker connected to that network, could read or even modify other users traffic. HTTPS to an extent can provide protection against some of this stuff on an open network, but OWE uses an unauthenticated Diffie-Hellman key exchange during that association, resulting in what's called a Pairwise Master Key, or a PMK. And they use that to derive, then the session keys, and that's unique to each user. Each user that connects gets that unique session key. There's no provisioning required, and the encryption process is entirely transparent to users. The users would see and join the Wi-Fi network as they would any typical open network as they've done in the past, but they don't have to do anything additional to get that encrypted connection. So OWE is a big improvement over current open wireless networks. Then just keep in mind, we use SHA-2 for each input. And then Wi-Fi Easy Connect is another big advancement that uses Device Provisioning Protocol Secure, or DPP Secure, and that will replace WPS, or Wi-Fi Protected Setup, so it makes things much easier. Using your smartphone, you would scan a QR code on that device and then automatically pair any new devices that would connect it to the network, so it makes provisioning much, much easier. Then lastly, WPA3 is not susceptible to the KRACK attack like WPA2 was. WPA2 was susceptible to something called the KRACK attack, which came out in roughly 2017, and it rendered WPA2 vulnerable. WPA3 is not vulnerable to that same attack due to the way they use Simultaneous Authentication of Equals, or the SAE key exchange.

Wireless Security Examples
Let's take a look at a real-world example of how a hacker could gain access in an environment. Let's say, for instance, we have our two wireless access points that we have. Well, if someone wanted to come in, they could set up what's called a rogue access point. They could issue a Denial of Service against our existing wireless access point, take it offline or make it so that it can't respond to requests. They could put a wireless access point using something called open authentication, which means there is no password required. The laptop, whoever's sitting at that laptop, they would connect to that wireless access point, otherwise known as an evil twin. That's a term you should be familiar with or you should remember. But an evil twin is there to fool someone connecting to the network. They think they're connecting to the wireless access point. Even though they have credentials to connect to the legitimate wireless access point, that's going

to be DDoSed so they can't connect. They're going to connect to the evil twin. It's using open authentication, which means they don't need a username and password to connect. They're connected. And if we are in control of that wireless access point, of that evil twin, we can set it so that it pops up some type of authentication message. The user sitting at the laptop would think, something must have happened; it's prompting me for my credentials. They'll go ahead and put in their username and password, or they'll do that several times. We just keep putting up fake messages until we capture enough information that we can be pretty confident that we have what we need off of that user. Then we can just disconnect and off we go. In that case, we could very easily compromise that communication. We could capture everything, or we could have it connected to the network and let them pass through and connect. We could just sit there and monitor everything that they do as that communication passes through the wireless access point. Just be advised that those types of things are, in fact, possible. You could be sitting at a coffee shop, and someone could do something similar to that. It doesn't necessarily have to be in a business environment. It could be anywhere that you would connect using a wireless access point.

Wireless Security and Pen Testing Tools

There is a number of off-the-shelf penetration testing, or pen test, tools that can quickly compromise insecure wireless protocols. We're talking about WEP and even WPA and WPA2. There are some tools, Kali Linux is one, or it used to be called BackTrack. There's some off-the-shelf scripts that can do packet injections and things that allow them to very quickly break those types of encryption protocols., what would happen is, it allows you to do network sniffing, Even if a specific wireless access point is not broadcasting, it's SSID. Even it's not broadcasting it can still sniff the wire because those things are being transmitted in the clear. Even though your laptop may not pick it up and say, hey, there's a wireless network available, it's still being broadcast, and if you have the tools, you can gather that information. It'll allow you to locate all the wireless networks and show what types of encryption they're using, what types of protocols, if they're open or secure, whether it's WEP WPA. And once you find one, you can then capture the packets on that network to capture the SSID. From there, you can send out what's called a deauthentication packet, or you can knock those clients off the network. By deauthenticating them, then they're going to reconnect pretty much away. As they're reconnecting, you're going to capture those packets, and you'll be able to capture the actual login. It's encrypted, but you'll be able to capture the packets and you can identify that as login attempts because it's what's called a four-way handshake as they reconnect. And once you have that information, then you can brute force your way in or dictionary attack or hash attack to discover that password. If it's something simple, you can get through that relatively quickly. If you're using more secure passwords or a stronger password with like uppercase, lowercase, special characters that wouldn't necessarily be in a dictionary, then it could take longer. It could take days, hours, weeks, months, just depends upon the strength of your password. Having said that, there are other tools available that can bypass even having to crack the password. Most routers, especially the home office and SOHO routers, have what's called WPS. It allows you to do a push button on either side and automatically configure the client and the server, or the client and the wireless access point, rather. There are insecurities or some vulnerability within WPS, the PIN that it generates, that it can go out and attack that at the wireless access point and crack the WPA or WPA2 password. There are some tools available that do not take an extreme amount of knowledge to utilize. You need to be aware of these things. You need to make your networks as secure as possible.

EAP, PEAP, and LEAP

The next sets of concepts I want to cover are EAP, or Extensible Authentication Access Protocol, and then two variations of that, PEAP and LEAP. EAP, or Extensible Authentication Access Protocol, is a set of authentication frameworks for wireless networks. What you need to understand is that there are five different types of Extensible Authentication Access Protocol that are in existence, two that we need to know for the exam that are adopted by the WPA and the WPA2 standard. We have EAP with TLS. We have EAP with Pre-Shared Key, and we have EAP with an MD5 hash. Those three have been deprecated. The two that we need to be aware of are LEAP and PEAP. Let's cover that in a little more detail. LEAP stands for Lightweight Extensible Authentication Protocol, and this one is not in use, but we need to be aware of what it is. It's a proprietary protocol developed by Cisco, and it was a stopgap to WEP insecurities, and it lacked Windows support. It was not in use or used by the Windows environment. It was strictly for Cisco environments. That itself is why it doesn't have the wide acceptance or it's been deprecated. It's easy to configure, no digital certificates, which is great. But it's also bad because it's easy to configure and there are no digital certificates. You have a lot of insecurities there. Clear text transmissions. And, it has since been deprecated. The one that we need to be focused on is PEAP, or Protected Extensible Authentication Protocol, and that was jointly developed by Cisco, RSA, and then Microsoft. Cisco develops the networking protocols. RSA deals with security. And then Microsoft with the operating systems. This joint effort ensured that it is in use or wide adoption throughout the IT and the tech community. It has Windows support, and it uses digital certificates on the authentication server. It gives you that extra layer of security by authenticating saying, I'm not going to just connect to any rogue access point, like we mentioned previously with that evil twin. If we're using PEAP, that will prevent that from happening. We have to authenticate to what we're connecting to, to the wireless access point and then ultimately to the server. It's going to establish an encrypted channel between the client and the server via a TLS tunnel. It gives us that extra layer of protection.

802.11x Wireless Protocols

Let's now talk about IEEE 802.11x wireless protocols. What we're talking about here is wireless communication and 802.11 standards operate either over 2.4GHz or the 5GHz radio frequencies. Over time, we've gotten an increase in speed for the most part, and we've gone from 1 Mbps or 2 Mbps up to 14 Gbps, theoretically. 802.11 was the original standard, and that was 1 Mbps or 2 Mbps, and that operated over the 2.4GHz frequency. Next was 802.11a, and that was a big jump. That was 54 Mbps over the 5GHz frequency. Then the next iteration of that was 802.11b, and that dropped down to 11 Mbps and operated over the 2.4GHz range. But wait a minute, that's a step backwards. Why are we doing that? Well the big difference between the two is the fact that 5 GHz has a much shorter range than 2.4 GHz. So for those devices that needed very high speed or high throughput, you could in fact use 802.11a, but the range was much shorter than it was with 802.11b. That's the big difference is the range. 802.11g, however, was a big jump up, and that gave us pretty much parity with 802.11a as far as throughput, 54 Mbps. But it had the advantage of operating over 2.4 GHz with an expanded range. Then we jumped to 802.11n up to 600 Mbps, again a huge jump, 2.4 or 5 GHz. Then, up until recently, 802.11ac was the latest and greatest with throughput up to 1.3 Gbps. That operated only over the 5GHz network. And we have 802.11ax, also known as Wi-Fi 6, and that can theoretically go up to 14 Gbps, although, in reality, probably a lot less than that, at least for. But as devices get better and the frequency range expands, we'll see speeds approaching that 14,000 Mbps or 14 Gbps. it operates over 2.4GHz or 5GHz range. You may also see something referred to as 802.11i. That's often referred to as WPA2, and that provides for additional security enhancements focused on authentication. But it does not refer to speed or frequency like the other things we just mentioned.

RADIUS Federation

A concept I want to make sure we're clear on is RADIUS Federation. We've discussed what RADIUS is, remote access dial-in user service, and federation is simply connecting systems or combining systems. A RADIUS federation connects a common system of authentication and credentials database. It uses RADIUS servers to connect these systems wirelessly. Additionally, because it's a federated system, it can be used by multiple applications or platforms.

Wi-Fi Protected Setup (WPS)

WPS is designed to make it easy for devices to join Wi-Fi networks with minimal effort. Devices without screens or keyboards are ideal for this. Some printers, as an example, they can easily join a Wi-Fi network by pushing a button on both devices, one on the actual printer, in this case, and then the access point on the other. Or some devices without that push button functionality will have a hardcoded pin, usually on a sticker somewhere on that device. Even though WPA2 encryption is used, assuming the actual wireless access point is using WPA2, it's very secure. As of the time of this writing, it has not been cracked. It's considered very, very secure. However, the WPS pin can be easily cracked. That pin is eight characters long, but only seven of those characters are used. The eighth character is a checksum. The first three and then the last four are in two separate groups. It ends up being fairly easy to brute force crack given the power of today's PCs.

Captive Portal
When we're dealing with public or open Wi-Fi networks, the concept of a captive portal comes into play. You may have been in a coffee shop or some location, a hotel, where you've attempted to log on to that Wi-Fi network and then you get some pop-up that says, before your able to access the network, you need to either agree to our acceptable terms of use, or you need to put in your username and password. It might be your last name and your room number or whatever if it's a hotel. Once you put in those credentials, then it allows you access to the network. That captive portal in quarantine or put you into a walled garden and say, you can't get any further until you authenticate. Once you do, then it allows you through, and you can have full access to the internet. Well, those types of things are vulnerable to different types of attacks, again depending upon the implementation. But one example would be packet sniffing. If a hacker sits on the network and is sniffing the packets, once you

authenticate, again, it just depends upon the sophistication of the captive portal and of the network itself or the tool that's being used. But if it's simply just looking for authentication by, like say, username and password, well, it knows your IP address, and it knows you're MAC address. Once you provide those credentials, it says you're authenticated, off you go. Well if someone is sniffing the network and they get your IP address and the MAC address, they could then, in turn, spoof both of those pieces and make it look like it's you. As soon as they hop on the network with that IP address and the MAC address, well the captive portal thinks that they're already authenticated, and it allows them to go through as well. That's one method. Or they could put up a fake captive portal. Again, if you're in some type of coffee shop, there may not even be typically a captive portal in place. But you, as the unsuspecting user, would not necessarily know that if you see a pop-up and says hey, you need to put in your username and password, 9 times out of 10, people don't think twice about it. They just go out and start putting those things in. Well those things could, in fact, again, be captured by someone sitting there just being malicious and capturing this information to get usernames, passwords, or whatever other things are trying to gain from a credentials point of view.

Installation Considerations

When it comes to installing Wi-Fi on our networks, some installation considerations to take into account. We can do things such as site surveys, which are a walkthrough of a facility to visually confirm locations, potential hotspots, impediments, maybe brick walls or some other things that could impede the flow of our signal. We can visually inspect those things to make sure that we have those accounted for. We can also generate things called heat maps, and that is typically done with software and some type of analyzer to visually show where signal is weak or non-existent you can add additional hotspots or access points. That's used in conjunction with Wi-Fi analyzers, that is, again, hardware and software that allows a tech to walk a site and identify areas of weak signal and what channels are best. It will show what devices are attached to what channels, which are better than others, and will allow you to switch channels potentially to find the best one for that specific device and improve the overall quality of the signal for a specific device.

Access Points/Wi-Fi Security

Let's now talk about some concepts around securing your network from things like access points, Wi-Fi security. So rule number one is to disable SSID broadcast. That's not a foolproof method. It doesn't mean someone still can't find you. But why give out extra information if you don't have to? Disable the SSID broadcast. It's the Service Set Identifier, the Wi-Fi network name, in other words. Also, it doesn't provide security. This SSID can still be sniffed. However, let's not give away too much information. Next, use something referred to as MAC filtering. We talked about a MAC address before, with MAC filtering, we pre-select what MAC addresses can connect to the Wi-Fi network. It still doesn't make it completely foolproof because people can do MAC spoofing just like they do IP spoofing. If they can sniff the network or if they explicitly know the MAC address ahead of time, it's possible to spoof that MAC address and then still connect to the network. Also, common sense administration. Always change the default admin username and password. I know it sounds ridiculous, but in all honesty, if you do a quick bit of research, you'll find that common usernames and passwords, literally password or password123 are out there, and they're very common, so people don't take the time to secure their networks. Also, we want to make sure we use the strongest encryption and authentication available. In other words, don't use WEP when we have WPA or WPA2 available. Keep things up to date and use the strongest encryption and authentication possible. Also, keep access points up to date with patches and firmware. There are a lot of home networks, small office networks, mid-sized companies, they install a router or Wi-Fi access point, and then they forget about it. They don't go back and touch it again. Make sure those default usernames and passwords are changed. Make sure they're locked down. Make sure you use the strongest encryption possible. But just like any other computer, any other device, make sure we keep things patched and updated. Next, we want to make sure we have antenna placement and signal strength flushed out. Antenna placement is critical for proper coverage, so it should be placed near the center of the area to be covered, and antennas can be internal or external. There is not one type that's better than the other. It depends upon the manufacturer, and it also depends upon the type of router. However, there are always new models coming out, and you can also add additional access points within a Wi-Fi network to extend coverage. Next, we have antenna placement and signal strength. Antennas can be omnidirectional or unidirectional. Omnidirectional provides coverage in a 360-degree fashion, whereas directional antennas focus the signal primarily in one direction, usually over longer distances. If you have an area where you want blanket coverage everywhere, then an omnidirectional antenna is your best bet. If you have somewhere where you want to broadcast coverage or direct coverage to one area but not to the sides or not behind you, as an example, then a directional antenna is your best bet. Something else to consider is antenna signal strength. Antennas are rated in terms of gain value or dBi numbers. A wireless antenna with a 10 dBi would be 10x stronger than a 0 dBi. Some routers, some wireless routers provide control over that. You can turn the power levels up or down, depending upon the environment. Some out-of-the-box routers may not have that functionality, but you can download hacked firmware that can give you that additional functionality. It's there, but it's not exposed via the common, out-of-the-box user interface. We can combine with site surveys to identify optimal placements. You can take devices and walk the site, and determine where the signal strength is going to be best. Additionally, you can also identify where there's going to be dead spots. You may need to position your antenna so that you account for those dead spots, or you may add additional access points to the network.

Band Selection/Width
When we're talking about Wi-Fi connected access, there are two main bands that you connect with. You have 2.4 GHz and also 5 GHz. 2.4 GHz was the earlier band. It's 100 MGz wide, and it spans from 2.4 GHz to 2.5 GHz. Just 14 channels and used by

many devices outside of just Wi-Fi collectivity, such as microwaves, baby monitors, Bluetooth, wireless video cameras. In reality, only channels 1, 6, and 11 are separated from each other with enough space or enough frequency in between to not overlap. That's an important consideration to keep in mind when you're doing channel selection, especially if you have multiple access points within the same building, or if you have neighboring Wi-Fi access points, perhaps from other companies or neighbors, and you want to make sure you're not overlapping and getting a diminished signal, not having frequencies overlap. In order to do that, you would pick channels 1, 6, or 11 to ensure that you have some distance between you and the next set of channels that you'd want to use. On the 5 GHz range, we have 25 10-MGz channels, and the bonding of channels is possible within the 5 GHz range. So 802.11n bonds 2 20-MGz channels, and also 802.11 ac bonds 4 20-MGz channels. 802.11n, would give you 40 MGz of bandwidth, 802.11ac can bond 4 20-MGz channels for a total of 80 MGz of bandwidth. If we look at this in a little more detail, the 2.4-GHz channel frequencies, channels 1, 6, and 11 are far enough apart, there's a 3-MGz space in between those channels, so they don't overlap. If you're looking for the spread that has the most channels without overlapping, these are the 3 that you should pick, 1, 6, and 11.

Fat vs. Thin Access Points and Stand-alone vs. Controller-based

Fat or thick access points have everything needed to manage wireless clients, so all the intelligence and all the management features are in fact built in to the actual client. Multiple access points need to be managed individually, so that's the downside. The upside is it's easy to install. It's great for small offices or small environments. We have everything we need. We don't need additional hardware. However, if we have multiple points as our environment starts to grow and we have more than one access point, they need to be managed individually. A thin access point is just the radio and the antenna and can be managed via a central switch. As you may have guessed, multiple thin access points can be managed and configured centrally. We have the benefit of being able to do everything at once from a centralized location. If we have a large environment or one that has many access points, that very quickly becomes an advantage. When we're talking about stand-alone versus controller-based, it's very similar to fat vs. thin. Stand-alone access points provide everything required to service clients. They do, however, have limited encryption, typically no load balancing, and no enterprise class functionality. Not to say that some don't, but typically we have less functionality, less features, less encryption than we do with controller-based. To compare and contrast the two, it's very similar when we're talking about stand-alone versus controller-based, it's very similar to fat vs. thin with regard to features and functionality and ease of management. One, it's very easy to set up, it's very self-contained, but it doesn't scale very well. Stand-alone access points are usually found in smaller environments. Typically much less expensive, a little bit easier to configure on one-by-one basis. But as we start to scale, that becomes a little bit unmanageable. For stand-alone controllers, well suited to smaller environments, contain everything needed to manage clients updates and patches, however, need to be done individually. That's where it starts to become unruly. If we have multiple access points, we don't want to have to go around and do that to every single one, especially if we have dozens or potentially hundreds depending upon the size of our environment, especially if we're in between multiple buildings and we have some type of geodispersement. Also no load balancing and limited redundancy. Also, we have limited IDS or intrusion detection functionality. Conversely, with controller-based, we have enterprise-level features and also scalability. Access points are configured and managed centrally. Again, as that starts to scale, that becomes a big deal. Updates and patches are distributed from a central location. It's much easier to manage at scale. Load balancing and redundancy also between access points. As we move throughout an environment, it has the ability to load balance or to find the best or the closest access point, the one that can service the client the best. Also, we have more full-featured IDS functionality. Something to keep in mind, the fat client or the thick client and also the stand-alone controllers very well suited to small environments or medium-sized environments that work well. However, as we start to scale, we want to able to manage things from a central location. In summary, we various cryptographic protocols and the underlying information for each. We talked about a number of authentication protocols, including the relatively new WPA3 and its associated authentication protocols and some of the benefits of WPA3. And we talked about the various methods and then installation considerations, including site surveys, heat maps, Wi-Fi analyzers, antenna placement.

Chapter 11 How to Implement Secure Mobile Solutions

In this chapter we'll be covering Implementing Secure Mobile Solutions. We'll be talking about connection methods and receivers, along with mobile device management, also enforcement and monitoring, and then deployment models. At a high level, we want to talk about connection methods. We want to talk about mobile device management concepts, also talk about enforcement and monitoring, and then also deployment models. There's a lot of information in each of these categories, and it's important to understand that we have a good concept or a good understanding of how these things tie into our overall security posture. Mobile connectivity is a big deal. Everyone is mobileadays, we have remote workers, teleworkers, so it's important that we understand how this fits into the big picture. Let's go ahead and dig in and talk about connection methods. There's a lot of ways that we can connect to our corporate networks. We can connect via cellular, Wi-Fi, SATCOM, not as common as some of the other ones, but for military installations, SATCOM is a big deal. Also Bluetooth, NFC or near field communication. We also have ANT or ANT+, which connects health devices and gym equipment. Also

Infrared and then USB. There's connection concerns and security concerns with all of these different methods of communication. If we take a look at each of these individually, there are some unique challenges that we face. To start off with cellular, cellular or mobile phones in general have numerous potential security risks, not the least of which, if we have a cell phone that we're carrying around in our pocket that connects to our corporate resources. If we have no password or no pin on that device, if we leave it somewhere, if it's lost, stolen, or somehow compromised, anyone could pick up that device and have access to corporate emails, corporate resources, or more depending upon what is on that device. It's important that we make sure all of our devices have passwords or pins, and we'll talk more about that later as far as mobile device management so we can force that. If someone's using a device to connect to our corporate resources, we can make sure that they do, in fact, have a password or a pin. Also, unpatched operating systems or applications. If people download applications to their phone, or even if we push applications out in a corporate setting, if we don't update those applications or update the operating system on the phone, it's just like any other operating system or any other application. The phone is no different or a cellular device or mobile device is no different than a PC, laptop, server. They need to be patched and updated periodically. Next, you have jailbreaking or rooting. It's very popularadays, especially with iPhones, to jailbreak that device or gain root access to that device so they can install their own applications. They can bypass the App Store, download things or increased functionality or turn on features that may not be readily accessible from the stock or the factory OS. Jailbreaking is a definite security concern for IT professionals or security professionals because those phones are no longer managed or manageable. Those phones are able to bypass our security settings, and they can install whatever they want. When you bypass the app stores, especially in the iOS space, those things are very well vetted. They have security guidelines and best practices they must follow to even be admitted into these App Store. When you bypass that and you go to your own app stores, these off-on-the-side jail broken app stores, people will create their own apps and add functionality that is not vetted as thoroughly as it would be in the App Store. You run potential security risks by having that in the environment. Then, we have unauthorized applications. They can either jailbreak the phone from the Apple Store perspective of the App Store perspective, whether it's Apple or Android, or they could install unauthorized applications from a company perspective, meaning the company says you can install applications A, B, C, and D, but the person goes in and installs their own applications. That could potentially bypass the security because IT security, again, doesn't know what ports they go over, what things they access, or what mechanisms they have in place that could potentially be a security risk. As an IT professional, we should mandate or have a list of what applications can and cannot be used on those corporate resources. Then last but not least in this category, everyone's favorite topic is malware. Malware is everywhere, laptops, PCs, desktops, servers, so on. It also exists in the mobile phone space or the cellular space. If you have a mobile phone, iOS is not as susceptible, but it still exists. Android much more so because it's more of an open environment. People can create apps not necessarily through a rigorous vetting process like they have in the Apple Store. But malware exists on both sides. Don't develop a false sense of security and say oh, I have an Apple device. I'm completely immune. There is malware. There are potential security risks with every device. Some methods to secure our mobile devices and our cellular communication in general would be authentication or two-factor authentication. We want to make sure that we authenticate. We put in a username and password. We want to make sure we have a pin or some type of biometrics, thumbprint or fingerprint of some sort, or a two-factor authentication. If we're going to go connect to a specific service, a lot of those services will offer a two-factor authentication. Typically that means they will send an SMS or a text to that phone, you'll need to have the password. Then you'll also need to verify that you're on the phone that was registered with that service. They'll send a password to that device via text. You'll put that text password back in, and that's the two factor. That way someone has to have your phone in addition to being able to try to access that specific resource. There are some other ones out there like context-aware authentication, which we'll talk about in a bit that offers a little easier experience, less friction involved. You don't have to have the device and go through an extra couple of steps by getting that pin or that text from the website or the resource to put back in again. We'll talk about those in just a minute as well. But then we want to also make sure that we verify and authenticate downloaded applications. We need to make sure that if we download something from the App Store or from the internet or from wherever that we have a mechanism in place to verify and authenticate that that application is authorized by the company, is not manipulated or somehow tainted or tampered with prior to delivery. Also, make sure we put in anti-malware software just like we have on a PC or laptop. We want to make sure we have anti-malware and antivirus software on those mobile devices. That way we capture the malware before it gets a chance to take a foothold within our system. Also, we have firewalls. It's a good idea to have a firewall in place if you're in an environment where the risks necessitate that. Everything we talk about within IT security in general, there's a risk/reward. There's a what's the chances of it happening? What's the actual damage if it occurs? What's the likelihood of it occurring? The annual loss expectancy and the single loss event. A lot of things go into play when we're talking about risk analysis. Does the amount of effort that's going to have to be put in place outweigh or justify the actual action? In other words, to put it another way, if we have to spend a thousand hours or say a million dollars for some type of security solution, but the actual thing that's preventing might only cost us 10 hours and maybe $1000 to remediate, well then it's not worth it. We have to have that risk return mentality. Then it goes without saying, we need to have the ability to do a remote disable and/or remote wiping. Most phones have that ability already built in for the individual users, and then there's a corporate or an enterprise mechanism that allows that as well. If that device is lost, stolen, compromised in some way, we can number 1 locate it. We can look on a map and geolocate that device. Or, at the very least, remote disable that device so they can't use it or remote wipe it. All the data is completely removed from that device. And then last but not least, we need to make sure we have encryption in place. That way, if for some chance, the remote disable or the remote wipe doesn't work or is inaccessible, well then we can make sure, at the very least, that the data is encrypted on that device. Someone would need to use a biometric mechanism like a fingerprint or username/password to get into the phone. They couldn't use a third-party tool to extract that data.

Securing Wi-Fi

When it comes to securing Wi-Fi, a couple main things that we should be aware of, and you're probably familiar with some of this, but just to reiterate, we need to make sure that we are disabling the SSID. None of these are foolproof, none of them are going to stop an experienced attacker from doing what they're doing. But disabling the Security Set Identifier, or the SSID, more skilled hackers from finding the network, but it will prevent clients who are just casually browsing from discovering your network. You're going to eliminate some of the casual ones that could eventually end up becoming problems. You're not going to eliminate the experienced hackers, however. Next is MAC filtering. MAC filtering predefines which Media Access Control, or MAC addresses, can connect to that router or that access point. it will not prevent a skilled hacker from spoofing that MAC address, but it does keep the casual browsers, the casual, lower-level hackers, or miscreants, or, whatever you want to call them, from attaching to your network, because you're going to say only these MAC addresses are allowed. If they're skilled, they will be able to spoof that MAC address and then connect anyway. And then, Require Security Connectivity Protocols, we want to make sure we're using the most secure protocol available. No WEP, no WPA. If it all possible, require WPA2-PSK with AES, or Advanced Encryption Standard. That uses a pre-shared key with AES. That's currently considered the most secure standard, there are some other ones you can do at enterprise level, but they have to contact a RADIUS server, or they have to have a certificate, but for the average user, especially for a home environment or a small office, a medium-sized environment, WPA2 with a pre-shared key using AES, make sure you don't use TKIP, use AES, that's considered most secure.

Near Field Communication (NFC)
Most commonly, we're seeing near field communications in use for things like contactless payment systems, the iPhones, Android devices, Apple Pay. All those types of things have the NFC

infrastructure in place, but it does pose some security concerns, things like eavesdropping, data corruption or manipulation, or interception. Just like with any communication, there's always that potential for a man-in-the-middle attack or someone to intercept that communication. With near field communication or NFC, they're hampered because of the fact that it's a very close-range technology. They have to be very close to you to be able to do any of those types of things anyway. However, that's not to say that someone can't sit next to or stand next to some type of payment checkout system and gather information, try to manipulate that data or intercept the communication. Don't just assume just because, I only have to be maybe a foot away that I'm safe. No, someone could be standing nearby or they could have some type of device placed nearby that could intercept that communication. Some ways we can prevent some of that is by establishing secure channels. If those secure channels are established and that communication is encrypted, then we thwart a lot of those efforts. Even if they do intercept that communication, they're not going to able to do anything with it because, that communication is encrypted.

Additional Areas of Concern

Some additional areas of concern are common attack vectors like intercepting data, man-in-the-middle attack, and data corruption. These things can apply to any type of communication interaction between two devices. Some additional areas of concern are common attack vectors that are common to any communication mechanism. Like intercepting data, man-in-the-middle attacks or data corruption. These things apply to things like satellite communications, Bluetooth, we're going to talk about Bluejacking and Bluesnarfing in another chapter, ANT or ANT+, which is the connection between health and gym equipment, heart rate monitors, and then infrared devices. We need to disable unnecessary or unneeded services and ensure that devices are patched, updated, and encrypt communication where possible. With things like satellite communication, there are some vulnerabilities. Some of them are embedded and maybe not easily upgraded, but it's important that we understand that every type of communication has its own unique challenges, and there are common exploits, or at least in concept, among all these different types of communication mechanisms. SATCOM used by government installations, military installations, very important that we keep those things patched and updated.

Make sure that we understand that vulnerabilities do exist. Just because it's a military grade, whatever, it doesn't mean it's impervious or immune to viruses, malware, and the targets or the information they're trying to get at. They would be considered typically high value targets. Bluetooth, if you don't need it for anything, turn it off because they are susceptible to things like Bluejacking and Bluesnarfing. But, as new devices come on board, smartwatches that have that connectivity, while there may be an opportunity for hackers to exploit that, currently not as much of a problem. Infrared, a lot of laptops, especially the older ones, have infrared built in. Some of the desktops have infrared built in. If you don't need that, which typically you will not, then turn that off because even though it's a line of sight communication mechanism, it is exploitable. It is vulnerable. You can use infrared ports to gain information or gain access to a system. Turn those things off. We want to harden our systems by disabling unnecessary things. Because the more things that are there, the more things that are exploitable. If we don't even know that they're turned on or we don't know that they're in play, then we're not going to monitor them, and they're going to fall out of compliance over time and then introduce additional vulnerabilities into our environment. Disable unnecessary services, harden our systems where possible.

MicroSD HSM

A MicroSD HSM offers the same features as PCIe-based HSM chapter that we find in servers. It can be used to encrypt communication, to encrypt storage, for key generation or for digital signatures. It can also provide, depending upon the type of card, it can also do true random number generation, provide TRNG functionality, and then also cryptocurrency use cases, we can use it as a cold wallet of sorts and encrypt those transactions. A MicroSD HSM can be used for all of these purposes, can be mobile, and be moved from device to device, and give the same levels of encryption and security that we find on servers and bring that to the mobile environment, assuming your device can handle a MicroSD card.

Mobile Device Management (MDM, MAM, and UEM)

Next let's talk about mobile device management, and three things here, we have MDM, or mobile device management being software that enables the provisioning of mobile devices, application of policy, remote wiping, and some security policies that we can push down via certificate to these mobile devices and provision them, whether it be a corporate owned device or a BYO device. Next, we have mobile application management, or MAM, and this is more granular control over mobile devices, especially BYOD Devices where policy enforcement can be set at the app level along with application containerization, meaning we can apply policy to a specific application, but not affect the rest of the applications on a user's device. We can even control what can be copied between applications on a device or if things could be uploaded to the cloud based upon policies pushed down from mobile application management software. Then we have unified endpoint management, or UEM, and this is an evolution of MDM EMM, which is enterprise mobility management, and also, MAM, or mobile application management. UEM combines the features of these different types of technologies along with being able to manage desktops, laptops, Internet of Things devices, pulling all of these different feature sets under one umbrella.

SEAndroid

Next, we have security enhanced Android, or SEAndroid, and this is an SELinux, or a security enhanced Linux kernel security chapter and its purpose is to provide a mechanism for supporting access, control security policies among other things, and when I say that, I mean things like mandatory access control where we mandate that things must happen in a certain fashion, it's not discretionary, it's mandatory, and it was originally developed by the NSA and released to open source in December of 2000, so it's been around for a while, and it's been part of the Android code base for quite a while as well. The takeaway here is it restricts actions that installed software can take with the end goal being to enhance security on that device. We all know the Android app store has some vulnerability issues, but guess what, Does the iOS app store, so there are vulnerabilities on both sides of the fence, so it's a bit of a religious argument as to which side or which camp you're in, but understand that both sides of the fence, whether it's iOS or Android, both try very hard to make things as secure as possible, and SE Android, or security enhanced Android, is one of the mechanisms put in place to help achieve that goal.

Device Security

Mobile devices pose a number of challenges? We've talked about some of those. What if that device is lost or stolen? What if it is compromised while on public Wi-Fi, or how about asset tracking? Do even know where all of our mobile devices are? Do we even have a mechanism to know if they've been lost or stolen, or perhaps going into areas where they shouldn't be going into? Do we know our mobile devices? Do they have applications that they're supposed to have or ones they're not supposed to have? And what mechanisms do we have in place to manage that and prevent that from happening? There are some ways that we can enforce that. Corporate policies need to be enforced. Let's start with policy-based enforcement, strong passwords, we're going to require that via policy. It's not just a recommendation, we're going to require it. We'll push it out with our mobile device management software, group policy if we're talking about Active Directory environment, we want to ensure that we're pushing out that strong password and/or a pin requirement. We want to make sure that we require lock screens and screensavers so that that phone is not used within whatever 30 seconds, a minute, minute and a half. Then that lock screen kicks in, or if it's a desktop or laptop, and then a screensaver kicks in. That way, if they walk away, we can be assured that that resource is secured. Then, disabling unnecessary services. This goes, of course, for iPhones and Android devices, mobile devices, in general, but it also goes for laptops and desktops. We want to make sure that we disable things we don't need. Then application and software control. We want to make sure that we have policies in place and mechanisms in place to make sure that only approved applications are installed and then software control so that the ones that are installed get updated and patched on a routine basis. Everyone knows there is nothing worse than reaching into your pocket, expecting to find your phone, and then all of a sudden, I've lost my phone, or you think you lost your phone You start searching everywhere, you start opening drawers, looking in your desk, and so on, all over the place, your heart stops, everything comes to a screeching halt and then you reach into your other pocket and realize, oh, thank goodness it's in my other pocket. And all of a sudden, everything is with the world again. All of our lives are wrapped up in our phones today, everything from personal information, banking information, personal photos to corporate access, corporate resources, and corporate emails. We want to make sure that we have these things locked down and secure, and we have the ability to remote wipe them or disable them if they're, in fact, lost. For device security, we want to make sure we have a few things in place. We want to have full device encryption, we want to make sure that the contents of that device are not able to be retrieved by an unauthorized person or persons, so full device encryption, even if they remove that hard drive or they connect that phone to some specialized device, we don't want them to have access to that data. Next, we have remote wiping. If in fact, that phone is lost or stolen, we want to have the ability to push a button and remotely wipe that device. Even if it's off the network, the command is issued, and then once that device attaches to the network, the remote wiping would take place. Next, we want to make sure we have GPS enabled or some type of location services, whether it's find my iPhone, or find my Mac, or some Android equivalent, we want to make sure that GPS is enabled We can see where that asset is geographically. We can geofence and say it's not allowed to leave this area, or if it goes into this area, please alert us, that way we can have secure areas that people should not be going into or we can pre-define areas they shouldn't leave and then be alerted, it goes both ways. And then we have mobile device management. In general, we need to have some software and some infrastructure in place to manage those mobile devices, and there are a few different ways to do this. We can either manage the entire device or we can cordon off a piece of that device, so if someone wants to use their own personal phone or their personal device, we can install MDM software on that device and cordon off a piece of that device for corporate use. That way, it's encrypted and it has remote wipe capabilities, and we don't affect the rest of that person's personal information of personal phone, but regardless of how you do it, mobile device management software is critical because we have people using mobile phones and mobile devices more frequently than they're using computers nowadays or laptops. Mobile devices are very much a part of our corporate infrastructure just as much, if not more, than PCs, so they need to be secured appropriately.

Application Security and Key Credential Management

When we're talking about application security, we want to make sure that we have such things as authentication, we need to make sure that applications are only allowed if they're authenticated, they are vetted either through some type of external process like an app store, or an internal process through our company. Some corporate process that says you're only allowed to install these 4, 5, 10 whatever applications, anything else is denied. Next, we also want to make sure we have geo-tagging. We want to have the ability to say this person is either in an area they're supposed to be or they're not, and if that phone travels in and out of an area or is lost or stolen, we can be alerted very quickly. Next will be biometrics, application security, we should have some method of requiring some type of biometric login for very secure applications. The iPhone has one built-in, Android devices are similar, where they have a fingerprint reader. Yes, you have a fingerprint reader to get in to the actual phone itself, but then certain applications require an additional level of authentication before the application will open. We can enforce that as well. Even if someone left their phone unattended and someone were to come by and pick that phone up while it was unlocked, they still couldn't get into those applications where we deem them to be highly secure, because they'll need that additional authentication like biometrics. Next, push notification services. If we have a large environment, it's going to be very unwieldy and certainly not scalable to have someone go around and talk to one person at a time and say, by the way, update your software; hey, by the way, update your software, and on and on and on, not scalable. In a small office, sure, we can stand up in the front of the room and say, everyone, update your iPhone or update your software. In an environment with multiple offices, thousands of employees, not scalable. Push notification allows us to push out to everyone in one shot, hey, update that piece of software, update that application, we can push notifications out across the board. We've talked about encryption. We want to make sure that our devices are in fact encrypted, and a lot of these things are built into the newer devices, so they become less and less of a of a management issue. The iPhone, Androids can be encrypted. IPhone by default is fully encrypted. That way, if the device is lost or stolen, it's a lot less likely that that information will be compromised, and also key or credential management. Let's take a look at that a little more deeply. With key or credential management, we want to manage the device content, access, and authentication. That is critical to providing a secure environment. The company needs the ability to manage the devices and control access. Digital certificates are often used to authenticate. It pushes down a certificate, so if you want to connect to the corporate resources, there is a certificate that's going to push down a profile to your phone, and it's going to mandate certain things. Maybe the screen saver will kick in or the device will lock after a certain number of minutes, or you can only access these specific types of applications, or you'll need this to connect and authenticate to our Wi-Fi; whatever the case might be. That way you have the ability to control with some granularity how people access and connect to your corporate resources.

Authentication

Then we're talking about authentication, securely connect to corporate resources. Again, we talked about PKI, that public key infrastructure helps to manage how people connect, and if they don't have the certificate, they don't have the authentication, they don't connect to our resources. Also, enforce password policies. We can make sure that people don't use the same password over and over again. We can make sure they change passwords every X number of days, let's say every 45 days. We can also enforce password history and also complexity requirements so that they can't use the same password, maybe say five passwords deep. That way they can't just reuse two passwords back and forth over and over again. We can also say their password has to have some type of complexity. In other words, it has to be maybe capital letters and lowercase, alphanumeric, or special characters or it may have to be a minimum length or a maximum length, so all of these things can help make our environment more secure. Then also, VPN or two-factor authentication. If they want to connect to corporate resources remotely if they're out in the field, coffee shop, they need to VPN in, and that way is over an encrypted secure channel. Even if that communication is, in fact, intercepted, it won't be readable to the hacker or to the person doing the interception. The VPN encrypts that communication. Then also, two-factor, RSA, as an example. Rather than just putting in a username and a password to connect to a VPN, you might have also a two-factor, which means they have to have an RSA token or some type of digital token that says every 30 seconds or every minute, this is going to change so that way the person trying to connect to that VPN, and ultimately to our corporate resources, needs to know their username and password, but also has to be in possession of that token or that two-factor device, whatever that might be. As an example, Google authenticator allows you to manage that two-factor authentication and for a number of services, Gmail, Dropbox, lots of different things can use Google authenticator to manage those keys, and of course, there are other companies, like I mentioned, RSA and a few others that can do the same thing.

Chapter 12 Geo-tagging & Context-Aware Authentication

Geo-tagging is important for a number of reasons. Pictures and documents can be tagged with the GPS coordinates of where it was made. A lot of people don't realize that when they upload pictures to social media, as an example, or they send that picture to others, there is a mechanism in place, it's called the EXIF data, E-X-I-F, if that data is not removed from that photo before it's uploaded, then that data is sitting there, and that person can use an EXIF tool to extract that information from that photograph. It's a potential security risk, as it allows someone to pinpoint that location. You can see here under the details, if you look down towards the bottom, it shows the GPS coordinates of where that picture was taken. The details being latitude and longitude, and also even the altitude of where that's at. Someone can punch in those coordinates and see exactly where that picture was taken. If it's a selfie with your girlfriend or boyfriend or whatever, probably not a big deal. But if it's a military installation and you're taking a picture of some type of battlefield location or government location, or something that has some type of security around it, and you don't realize this and you upload it to whatever, Instagram, social media, send it to someone else, and that other person uploads it to some social media, and that picture gets passed around versus text or instant message, or some other mechanism, that EXIF data is there. That is potentially a big security risk. There's software that can be used to remove EXIF data before things get uploaded, that comes down to corporate policy. You can have a policy in place that says, any photo that needs to be uploaded to any social media should have that information removed. That way it can't be pulled off for any reason.

Context-aware Authentication

Next, you have context-aware authentication. This is a type of two-factor authentication or 2FA, that provides for a more "frictionless" experience. It uses pre-defined rules to determine authentication, or if a more stringent challenge should be used. What do I mean by that? We can set it up to be based on things like device fingerprinting, geo-location, geo-fencing, or geo-velocity. What that means is when you register that device, it's going to look at the device itself. Where are you located? Are you East Coast, West Coast in the US? Outside of US? Where are you on the globe? Also, device fingerprinting. Let's say for instance it's a laptop. Well it can look at your browser, it can look at what fonts are installed, the browser version, drivers, screen size; all these different things that are unique, and when you combine all of those things together, it makes your device very unique against all others, because nobody has exactly the same thing; software, fonts, applications, security settings, screen size, color, depth. All those things go together to make a fingerprint, so that could be one thing. Also geo-location, like I mentioned, where are you located? Geo-fencing. Are you going to leave or enter a certain location? Or geo-velocity, meaning who checked in at say 2:00 in the afternoon on the East Coast, and then you're accessing the same website from 3:00 on the West Coast; that geo-velocity means, it's not feasible that person could've traveled across the country in an hour, or three or four hours. It's not feasible, so it would deny access. What happens is you can automatically allow things to occur if those things met, it's the same IP address or the same device fingerprint, or the same geo-location; you can allow them to just get in with the username and password. Or you can say if they fail any one of these pre-defined rules, then I want to challenge them additionally. Then you might ask for a pin, a two-factor authentication, an SMS text be issued or something. That way, it's frictionless up to the point where it can't verify via this context or authentication mechanism, I'm going to challenge you with some other thing, and then if they pass that, they're given access. If access fails any of the pre-defined rules, then the user can either be denied access out and say, nope, you don't gain access, or, we can be prompted for that more stringent authentication.

Enforcement and Monitoring

When it comes to enforcement and monitoring, there are number of things we need to be aware of, and I'm just going to touch on these briefly just you're aware that they exist and you have to make sure you keep eyes on these things. And that's things like third-party app stores. You have to make sure that our devices are not jailbroken or we restrict access to third-party app stores. We only want the people going to either the app store from Apple or Android, Google. Or we may have an internal company app store and only allow the applications we want them to have, and we would deny access to every other app store or every other download possibility. Next, also rooting in jailbreaking. We need to understand that people will try to root and jailbreak phones. When they do that, they're going to bypass security mechanisms. We need to make sure we have things in place to detect when those devices try to connect to our network and deny access. Also side-loading, custom firmware, carrier unlocking, or firmware over-the-air updates. All of these things should be prevented by corporate policy so that people can't bypass our security. We should make sure we have things in place. If we're going to have a corporately managed mobile policy and mobile infrastructure, we need to also make sure we have the corporately managed enforcement mechanisms so they if any of these things happen, people try to do their own firmware updates outside of what the corporate policy allows, they try to do carrier unlocking, any of those things should be denied and alerted so that we can go back and investigate further. Why is this person trying to do this? Also, we have camera usage. Some areas don't allow camera use on the phones, so they'll have them either disabled or they require phones without cameras, which is becoming more and more difficult nowadays. Pretty much every phone has a camera, but we can disable that so that people can't take pictures inside of our secure locations. Also, we have SMS or MMS. You want to make sure you understand how those things are being used, understand the security implications. People can text pictures, they can text PDF documents, they can text screenshots of data. It's up to each individual company, do you want to allow or disallow SMS and MMS. Also we have external media. We want to have policies in place to either allow or somehow restrict that external media usage, flash drives, USB drives, thumb drives. Do we want to allow people to be able to plug in and copy data or not? And then we have USB OTG or on the go. This is where USB devices, typically you have a PC and then say a disk drive, a master/slave configuration. Well USB on the go allows both devices to change roles. You can have two devices that typically wouldn't connect with each other be able to connect, and one takes the master, one takes the slave role, and transfer data between the two. There's potential to take a USB drive and plug it into a non-PC device or vice versa and transfer data back and forth. Do we allow that, or do we not allow that? And then recording microphones, that can be a big one. People could potentially go in and turn on a microphone on a laptop or turn on a webcam or so forth and record information without the person knowing. Actors will do that all the time, not to mention people intentionally doing it. You could have someone sitting in a meeting and turn on, record on their laptop, record the contents of that meeting. You may or may not want to allow that depending upon your environment. If in fact that's an issue for your environment, then you can disable that via policy. And we have also GPS tagging. We want to make sure that people are aware, and some of this is with training, that people are aware that GPS tagging exists with photos, with documents, so that they understand what is applicable. They understand what's advisable to send and not send and also the security implications when they do these types of things. And then also policies in place for things like Wi-Fi direct or ad hoc. We want to remove any rogue devices from our network. We want to scan for that and have infrastructure in place that detects when rogue devices are connected. We can even have it set up so that it scans for the manufacturer address. The first half of the MAC address defines the actual manufacturer. We can have policies in place that goes out and scans the network so that if someone were to plug in a Linksys or an ASUS or NETGEAR router, we can scan for those things. In other words, everything in our environment is, say, Cisco, we could scan for any non-Cisco routers or access points connecting. And if that happens, immediately shut that part down, send out an alert, and then have security investigate further. And then we have tethering. Do we allow devices to tether or not to tether? In other words, can someone take a laptop that doesn't have a cellular device inside and tether that to their phone? But that could be potential security risk because someone can then copy the data or send the data from their laptop over a carrier device that's not being monitored through our corporate infrastructure. There are potential security risks involved with that. It's a company choice whether we want to allow that or not. WE also have payment methods. Payment methods are one that has some potential for abuse, If we have the ability to do that in our environment, we need to make sure we secure those resources especially well because that's a big target for hackers and thieves.

BYOD Concerns and Deployment Models

Next we have BYOD concerns, BYOD or bring your own device. That's great for employees because it allows personal choice. You can have whatever device you want and use that in our corporate environment. It's a security challenge, however, for employers because they need to understand the nuances of many different platforms, patch management, lifecycle management. If we have two or three phones that we manage, it is very easy to understand what needs to be managed, the lifecycle of each of those devices, how to patch them, how to keep them updated. If we have 30 different devices, especially if we don't have that exact device in house, then there's nuances to that device that we're not aware of. It's important that we understand how those things function, how they need to be patched. BYOD challenges occur with monitoring, patch management, security leaks, access to data. It saves the company money. They don't have to invest in all of those mobile phones and mobile devices. But there's a trade-off. It comes down to personal choice. As a company, you need to decide which method is best for you. And then we have COPE, corporate owned, personally enabled. This bridges the gap by providing corporate-owned resources that employees can use for personal tasks. Some companies will give you a corporate device and say you cab only use this for corporate work, for corporate endeavors. More and more companies are saying we'll give you a device, we'll give you a phone. You can use it for whatever you want, but understand that we're going to monitor it. We're going to take ownership of it. We have the ability to remotely wipe it whenever we want if you feel that's lost, stolen, compromised. We own that device. There's trade-offs. It bridges the gap, but doesn't necessarily reduce costs because you still have to buy all the devices. But it also keeps people from bringing in their personal devices, so it gives you the ability to manage a little more tightly, but still allow them to use the device for personal tasks. And then we have CYOD, which stands for choose your own device. Again, a variation on the same concept. You have, say, five different devices that you can choose from. It gives them some choice, but the company owns that device, and it's still used and managed and falls under that corporate policy. And then we have two other deployment models. One is corporate owned, and that's the traditional. The company owns the equipment, and they dictate and monitor everything about that piece of equipment, what applications are installed, how it's used, how it's accessed, and, of course, they monitor everything. It also incurs the biggest cost to the company because they have to buy everything. Then we have also VDI or virtual desktop infrastructure. This is where a company provides a thin client to a user where the actual desktop resides on a centralized server. The device or the thin client that the person uses, it can even be a remote desktop session on a full-blown laptop. It doesn't necessarily have to be just a thin client. But the end user uses some mechanism, thin client or RDP connection, to a VDI server, and their actual desktop is then brought up on that VDI server. The nice part about that is all the desktops are essentially managed. They can be patched very quickly. They can be updated and also monitored or shut down or new instances spawned very quickly. That works great in instances where you have a lot of remote workers, perhaps contractors, offshore resources. You can give them a VDI instance very quickly, and then you can either maintain persistent desktops or non-persistent, non-persistent being every time they log on, they get a brand new desktop just like it's the first time they've used it. It will have the applications that they need, but it's a fresh install. Or you could have a persistent desktop meaning when they save things on their desktop, they save the configuration, the look and feel, that stays. That way when they log off and they log on the next day, all of those things, all of these changes they made the modifications will stay. That's better for developers and people that have a lot of customizations that they need. Otherwise, if you have, like, say, teleworkers or telemarketers or people that just do very repetitive tasks that they don't have any specialization or customization needed, then that non-persistent desktop works just as well.

Additional BYOD Concerns

Some other BYOD concerns, just something to think about, is data ownership. When you have people bring their own devices, who owns the data on that device? Again, all of these things should be called out in policy. People should sign off on this. They should read through your policies and sign off when they agree to connect their personal device to the corporate network. There should be some language and definitions around data ownership. Then next we have support ownership. Who's going to support the device if something goes wrong? Patch management. Who's going to push patches out? Is it the user, is up to them to do it, or is the company going to push patches out to make sure that it maintains a certain level to connect to that corporate resource? Same thing with antivirus management. Also, forensics. Do they have access to the entire device, to only a piece of the device, or do they have access at all? Again, it should be called out within your corporate policy. When it comes to privacy, does the user have any expectation of privacy? If it's a corporately owned device, they don't. But if It's a personally owned device, and they're attaching to corporate resources, there needs to be a clear definition of what is considered private data and not. That's where mobile device management software comes into play. You can cordon off or restrict or containerize a piece of that phone for corporate use, and everything else stays outside of corporate purview, in theory. And then we have onboarding or offboarding. What policies, what training does someone have to go through when they join a company, and then also, when they leave a company? Next, adherence to corporate policies. They have to read a policy that says, you're going to adhere to our policies. It seems a little redundant, but you as a company need to make sure your policies are in place and then also make sure the person has read those policies and agrees to them. Otherwise, they shouldn't have access to that corporate resource. And that leads into user acceptance. You need to make sure they read the policies and then accept. Also, infrastructure considerations. What infrastructure is required to support these BYOD devices? If I allow someone to bring whatever model and version of a device they want and connect to our resources, connect to our corporate environment, should I, as the company, also have a copy or a duplicate of that device? If it's a Galaxy, whatever, S8 as an example, do I need to have an S8 on hand so I can support, understand patch management and lifecycle management of that device. That's, again, cost considerations. And then legal concerns, the legal considerations around acceptable use, which we have here, things they can and can't do, places they can and can't visit, who owns the data, support, and all these things fall under that acceptable use policy. Then last but not least, on-board cameras and on-board videos. In most environments it's not a big deal, but if you're a government installation, a highly secure environment, a factory or a plant, maybe it has highly explosive chemicals, or is potentially a valuable target for hackers or terrorists or, cyber criminals, organized crime, then as a company, you may say, I don't want anyone taking any video or any pictures inside of our environment, maybe inside of a data centre. All of those things need to be spelled out in our acceptable use policies, signed off, reviewed by legal, and signed off by the individual before you gain access to the network. In summary, we covered four main topics at a high level. We talked about connection methods. We talked about mobile device management concepts. Also talked about enforcement and monitoring. And then we talked about deployment models, keeping yourself and your workforce secure while on the move or at a remote location.

Chapter 13 How to Apply Cybersecurity Solutions to the Cloud

In this chapter, we'll be talking about Applying Cybersecurity Solutions to the Cloud. We'll be talking about cloud security controls, talking about high availability, and the subcomponents, including storage, network, and compute. We'll talk about various solutions, like a cloud access security broker, or CASB. And we'll also talk about Secure Web Gateways, among other things, along with cloud native controls. As we start talking about cloud and cloud security solutions, we need to define what's the main reason or one of the main attraction points to going to the cloud. Security is one component, but also high availability. Let's talk about high availability across zones. What we'll see here is that we have availability zones or failure zones. We have a primary site which will be on-prem in this example, and then a failover sight that lives in the Azure cloud. We have duplicate resources, if you will. So high availability ensures that a resource (and whether that's an application, a service) remains available even when some of the subcomponents fail, whether it be network, storage, compute. We need to architect to make sure that if any of those things fail that we have failover capability to able to move that over to alternate infrastructure. Most cloud providers can enable HA across various pieces of infrastructure when initially creating or after installation. You don't necessarily have to pick that choice away; it can be instantiated after the fact in most cases. Applications need to be architected properly, however, to take advantage of these failover capabilities. It's not magic, we don't just pull a legacy application from an on-prem or something that's old or oldish, it could be a year old, but that's ancient in IT times, things move so fast. A legacy application, you can't just necessarily take it from on-prem, drop it in the cloud, and magically it's HA. It has to be architected to take advantage of failover capabilities, and wherever possible, have the data abstracted above the infrastructure layer, that persistence lives at the application, not necessarily the failover between the subcomponents - storage, compute. If we architect it properly, we could pull a server in and out, and the end user should not even notice. In this case we have resources that are grouped into what's called availability zones, which can be in the same data center, that's not optimal, but it's possible, we could have like four corner redundancy, as we call it. But what we talk about when we're saying availability zones is to have them in separate locations. That way, if one area goes down, even if a datacenter goes down, we can failover to that alternate facility very quickly, and keep things up and running.

Resource Policies

Resource policies enforce organizational standards and compliance. It can also control access to resources and allow access and control what actions may be performed. Not just allowing access to a facility or to a location or to a specific application, but then at a very granular level, say what specific actions can be performed. Also, what types of resources are allowed? Examples are what size VMs could be created. As an example, you might have a self-service portal or a service catalog for your end users where they can spin up resources. While you can set policy to say you have T-shirt sizes, you can have a small, medium and a large - the different sizes and what that means, it will be different for each organization. There is not one size fits all. But by implementing these resource policies, you can deploy and manage your resources in a very standardized way, the one-off applications, the one-off server, or infrastructure, or switch that's not like everything else and it needs to be cared for, managed differently than every other piece of infrastructure. The more we have standardization, the more we have things identical, then the less we have to troubleshoot. If something goes bump in the night, we can pull that out, put a new piece of infrastructure in. You know exactly how it's configured because they're all the same, and it can reduce our troubleshooting time quite drastically.

Secrets Management

When we're talking about the cloud and we're talking about DevOps, secrets can be thought of passwords, keys, APIs, tokens used for applications. The tools and methods for managing digital authentication credentials, secrets. It's just another word for digital authentication credentials. Some things to keep in mind with proper secrets management. Let's take a look at that. Proper and secure storage is critical. Cloud providers offer native secrets management tools. AWS has something referred to as Secrets Manager, Google Cloud Platform has KMS, or Key Management Service, and Azure has something called the Key Vault. There's also third-party secrets management platforms, such as CyberArk, and also HashiCorp has one called Vault. It's critical to have those things properly secured and not stored with your code. It's possible that unauthorized people could have access to those credentials. A few best practices are using resource policies and secrets management to enforce standards and also compliance. Best practices would be to authenticate all access requests that use non-human credentials, APIs. Also, enforce the principle of least privilege. We've always advocated for that in an on-prem environment. It's even more critical when we start talking about cloud and cloud resources. We need to make sure that we have the least privilege necessary People can access and do what they need to do, but not Much that that access can have unintended consequences. Also, enforce role-based access control, or RBAC, and then regularly rotate those secrets and credentials. The ones that I mentioned from Azure, from Google, and from AWS, they have auto rotation capabilities, so it's not something that you necessarily manually have to do; it can be done programmatically. Then also, automate the management of those secrets, and then apply consistent policies. Whether it's on-prem, whether it's on the cloud, or whether it's between multiple clouds, you might be a multi-cloud environment, make sure those policies are consistent across the board, and then track access and also maintain a comprehensive audit trail. It's very important to able to audit and then also go back if something happens to be able to go back and see what exactly happened and why. Remove secrets from code, from configuration files, and from other unprotected areas to make sure that that stuff is not there. So following those best practices will go a long way to making sure that's secure and keeping it from unintended access when in the cloud.

Storage in the Cloud

When it comes to storage, whether it's on-prem or in the cloud, there's three main options, and this pertains to the cloud, as well as on-prem. We have block storage, which can be thought of as local disk? It's either SAN Fibre Channel, or iSCSI. So from a host point of view, that storage appears as a local disk. And then we have file, which is network attached storage, and that's going to give you either CIFS, or SMB, or NFS. Whether it's a Windows box or a Linux box, typically you'll have CIFS or NFS or SMB and NFS. Then we have object, which is relatively new. That's synonymous with S3, although that's not the only object protocol. But S3 is the main one that everyone knows about and most people design, too, so that stores data as objects. It has objects, the metadata about that object, and a GUID. Those three things are stored together in buckets. When it comes to storage and making sure that things are secured properly, a couple things to keep in mind. We want to make sure that we define and then also audit who has permissions to the storage, and, the actual infrastructure as well, not just the file shares or the exports, the actual physical hardware of the infrastructure, or the virtual hardware, but the underlying infrastructure, not just what's exposed to the end user, along with the files and folders, objects. Then encryption. We want to make sure that the data that needs to be encrypted is encrypted, whether that's encrypted at rest, whether it's hardware or software-based; hardware-based will typically give the best performance, software-based usually will have overhead. Then key management. If we need encryption, it's important to understand what impact, if any, that encryption will have on the performance of the disk. Because in some instances, depending upon the piece of infrastructure, encryption can place an extra load on that data. And then also key management. Are they self-encrypting drives? You have a third-party key management platform? All of these things need to be taken into consideration when designing and architecting your encryption strategy. And then replication. Will the data need to be replicated, either on-site between arrays within the data center or within a location, or off-site? Are you replicating to a remote location, are replicating to the cloud? All of these things have funding implications. Then retention policies will also have an impact on the amount of storage required, the funding required. Then we have data sovereignty. If we replicate that data out of a specific location, perhaps a specific geographic location, are there data sovereignty implications? It's important that we understand those things. Then also, when we replicate, are we replicating to a read-only copy, making it perhaps an immutable copy to guard against ransomware? Or is it going to be a fully read-write copy, more of like in an HA environment? And then, we have high availability. High availability costs, location, additional requirements, such as network and compute, the architecture of the application may need the change, so all of these things should be taken into consideration when you're designing your storage, architecting your needs, and just understanding general implications around funding, the amount of infrastructure you need.

Virtual Networks

When we're talking about moving our infrastructure to the cloud or instantiating to begin with, maybe we're starting net new in the cloud, the networks that we'll set up are going to be virtual networks. Virtual networks are created much like physical networks, it's the same concept, the same layout. It's designed to segment traffic and secure communication. Virtual infrastructure is created for various roles. We can have things like load balancers, NAT devices, network address translation devices, traffic managers, Quality of Service, or QoS, managers, also firewalls and secure zones. All of the things that we would see in a physical world or physical infrastructure, there are virtual counterparts, and those things are typically set up in a self-service fashion when we're talking about cloud infrastructure or cloud resources. As an example, imagine if we have a virtual network, this is an example of a virtual network in an AWS instance, or an Amazon Web Services instance. A Virtual Private Cloud, or a VPC, is set up, and as an example, we have a internet gateway, we have a NAT gateway, we talked about that before, a bastion host, which is otherwise known as a jump server. That gives us something to remote into to then access infrastructure behind the firewall. Also the concept of availability zones, we have availability zone 1, 2, and 3, and these are set up to provide us with failover capabilities, whether it's HA or just failover in general, so that if one instance goes down, or one piece of infrastructure goes down, we can failover to another availability zone. That gives us resiliency and makes sure that our applications continue to run even if individual components fail. Availability zones, and then you also see we have public and private subnets, public subnets meaning things that are accessible to the public, private subnets meaning things that are behind a firewall or behind some type of gateway, and then the concept of segmentation, we're segmenting our network, public and private. We're also doing segmentation to give us additional failover capabilities, to reduce chatter, to segment, perhaps, different types of infrastructure or different groups, maybe one group should not talk to or should be cordoned off from another group for security reasons ? You have a number of different components here that we're talking about, but all of these things are set up virtually. They're all set up via a self-service portal when you instantiate within, whether it's AWS, or Azure, or Google, or any of the cloud providers, they have these self-service capabilities that allow you to click a few buttons, and then turn on this infrastructure. It's very convenient. You can provision infrastructure and resources very quickly, and duplicate what you could do, or what would take weeks or perhaps months in a physical world, if you have to go through acquisitions, and RFPs, and then go through your supply chain, and go through all the different hoops that you would typically have to go through to have infrastructure provisioned, you can do in a matter of minutes in the virtual world.

API Inspection and Integration
APIs being, application programming interfaces. A Gartner report recently said that by 2023, over 50% of business to business, or B2B, transactions will be performed via real-time APIs. What that means to us as security professionals is that securing those APIs is going to become more and more important, critically important as things go on, because more and more businesses will be conducted, not necessarily through a GUI front end, not necessarily through any type of human interaction, but through

APIs, so if those things are compromised or not secured properly, that could lead to some pretty catastrophic results. Just to give you some examples of how things can be secured, so here we have a user that will send a request, they're going to click on something, but behind the scenes, it's going to be connecting through to an API. So the raw request goes through and then we have things set up that will parse through that request and make sure that it's valid. As it parses through that request, it then takes the key and value representation and runs it through a filter in real time to identify all the things that are being passed through the API. Before it reaches its destination, it's going to go through a parser that then goes through it line by line and says, this is valid, this is valid, this is valid, and you'll see as it goes through it may identify something that's malicious or not constructed properly, and it will deny that. This type of security mechanism you can almost think of as a firewall for an API. It allows things to pass through that are valid, but it will parse through each individual piece of this, and if it finds something that's not legit, or malicious, it will block that request.

Growth of Enterprise Cloud Application
We have user-led, business-led, and IT-led. The reality of it is, again, according to some recent reports, is that roughly 30% of enterprise apps are

user-led, about 68% are business-led, meaning roughly about 98% of the cloud applications are led by either business or by users. Only about 2% or maybe a little bit less than 2% are led by IT. What that means is if IT is not in the loop, we have a lot of shadow IT possibilities, a lot of things that can go around IT, so it's important that IT get in the middle of this so they can become the broker to make sure that things are secured properly because if it's business-led or user-led, what's their goal? They want the application, they want the usability, they want the functionality of that application, they're not necessarily thinking about the security implications, so it's important that IT get out in front of this and not be a gating factor because if IT or if security makes things too difficult, what happens? Users just find a way to go around it, we have to make sure that we get in front of it, but we're also an enabler of that technology, not as a service? If we constantly say no, that won't work, you can't do this, you can't do that, can't do this, they'll just stop asking and they'll find ways to get around us. They'll pull out their credit card and they'll just buy the app or they'll provision it via some Software as a Service or a cloud app and we never even know about it. It's important that all these things tie together and that IT gets in front of these things.

Cyber Kill Chain in the Cloud

Cyber kill chain was developed by Lockheed Martin back in 2011. It's based on the military concept of a kill chain. If you understand how things work like the steps that an attacker would need to get from beginning to end and you understand the different points within that process, then you can develop defenses. Like any chain, if you break a link, then the chain falls apart. What we're doing here is looking for ways to break the links in that chain. Starting off, we have recon. When we're doing recon, it's probing for a weakness, harvesting login credentials or info that can be used for a phishing attack, as an example, and when we're talking about the cloud, publicly available information on company staff, executives, LinkedIn, Facebook, social media networks give out a lot of information. The reconnaissance process allows them to garner a lot of information about their subject. And then we talk about weaponization, step two in the cyber kill chain. Weaponization is creating the deliverable, a deliverable payload, using an exploit in a back door. Based upon publicly accessible information, a lot of times it's easy to create or easy to craft a message, whether it's malware, spyware, ransomware, we could put that in a malicious piece of email, a phishing attack and craft it so that it's very, very specific to the user, we're weaponizing and delivering that payload. Next is delivery. Sending the payload to the victim, a malicious email was quite often the attack vector, but often vulnerable users are discovered via social engineering and publicly available information. Also, Cloud services start to make this more and more efficient because the URLs, certificates are familiar to the user. If they have their weaponized payload delivered via a cloud hosting platform, that URL is familiar to the user, they don't necessarily look at it and question it, they just see I know what that is, and they click on it and then it gets delivered. Next, we have the exploit, so that's executing code on the remote system. Cloud services make this more effective or easier to exploit because popular cloud services are typically whitelisted, so they're allowed to get through the firewalls a lot of times. Instance awareness would help mitigate this step because the platforms and the tools we have that are instance aware can differentiate let's say, a corporate Gmail, or a corporate cloud services account, and a personal cloud services account, so you can allow some things through and not others, rather than just whitelisting everything. Next, would be installation. Installation is installing malware on the target asset. Again, with many cloud providers being whitelisted, this allows attackers to typically evade detection. Instance awareness, again, I'm mitigating control. If we can identify what's corporate and what's personal, we can block the personal accounts, so anything that an attacker would use as an example would be deemed personal or not corporate so it will be blocked, but it would still allow internal users to access these cloud services because it would be identified as a corporate resource. Next, you have command and control and this CNC is creating a channel and persistence where the attacker can control the system remotely. The cloud is great, but it has the potential to make things a little bit easier for the attackers as well, so cloud services make this challenging due to them being trusted in many environments and many popular applications can assist in masking that communication channel. They can use those communication platforms that are typically allowed in an organization, they can use them to deliver their payload and a command and control back and forth. Then we have the action in the cloud, persistence becomes more problematic because the attackers can move laterally across cloud services, they can escalate privileges, potentially encrypt data, or take services offline, they can also steal data or exfiltrate, and then instantiate new instances of cloud resources for things like crypto mining or crypto jacking, a distributed Denial of Service, botnets. It's important that we understand the steps in the kill chain, and then we develop defenses and then break the link in that chain somewhere along, the earlier the better, before it gets to step seven. They're getting what they came for.

Compute in the Cloud

When it comes to compute in the cloud, we have the concept of security groups, so controls like IAM, or Identity Access Management, things like secrets management, which we talked about, ACLs, or access control lists, and the concept of least privilege all become even more important with cloud resources. And why is that? Well, in the cloud, we have a much bigger attack surface. Cloud-based resources and cloud providers are, of course, big targets for hackers. And also, we have the concept of multi-tenancy. We have multiple clients that exist in the cloud, and that gives attackers a much wider berth to go after. You may not even be the target of a specific hack or a specific intrusion or breach, but if you're on the same infrastructure or shared infrastructure with other applications that are managed by groups or organizations that are the target of a breach, then you could potentially be impacted as well. So keeping all of these different pieces of the puzzle secure, as you can imagine, become even more and more important. Then we have the concept of a dynamic resource allocation. With the cloud, one of the big benefits and one of the attractive value props, or value propositions, is the ability to spin up resources on demand, but that also brings security, automation, and cost implications if not managed properly. In other words, if we spin things up and then forget about them and they just run, and run, and run, well, it does the bill. That gets higher and higher as well. Also, automation. If we spin things up and don't necessarily check it, and it just runs, and runs, and runs, and perhaps creates instances or creates load, or test, or whatever the automation is set to do, again, every time we run any process, we use any CPU, any cycles, any ingress or egress of data, all of those things incur costs. We need to make sure that someone's looking at those things, audits them periodically, and generally make sure that things are architected correctly and that we're not using too much resources because one of the whole benefits of the cloud is that we don't need to buy all the infrastructure up front. We need just as much as we need for that specific purpose, and then we can scale as required. The corollary to that being we tear the things down when we don't need them anymore so those costs don't continue to increase. Then we have instance awareness, understanding the differences between personal, corporate, and partner instances of cloud services, and then apply security policies accordingly. Instance awareness is a technology that's incorporated in some secure web gateways, next gen secure web gateways. It's an understanding of the difference between a personal account and a corporate account. A user at a company could have a personal and a corporate version of a cloud service. Typically, those things get whitelisted because you need access from the corporate side. However, if that user has a corresponding personal account, that would get through as well. That gives the opportunity or the potential for them to save things to their personal account, bring things in from their personal account. With an instance-aware technology, you can differentiate and block certain things that you don't want to get through. And then we have the concept of virtual private cloud, or VPC. A VPC endpoint, the same thing we talked about before. All of these different things, IAM, secrets management, ACLs, concept of least privilege, all of these things become more and more important for all the reasons we talked about previously. VPCs, or virtual private clouds, they're very, very convenient, they give us our own little mini data center, in the cloud. All of the things that we would take into consideration when designing a real data center, we need to make sure we do so in the cloud as well, and even more so because I said we have a multi-tenant environment where we have other companies and organizations that are sharing infrastructure with us, so security becomes important across the board. You're not controlling just your piece of the puzzle. Then container security, very much the same concept as dynamic resource allocation. We can spin things up on demand, but in doing so, we bring about security and automation and cost implications. If things are not managed properly, then we have the potential for costs to spin out of control or at least become larger than we anticipated.

Cloud Access Security Broker (CASB)

A Cloud Access Security Broker, or a CASB, it's a security policy enforcement tool or mechanism. It can be either on-premise or it can be in the cloud, and it's placed between the company or the consumer and the cloud provider. It ensures policies are enforced when accessing cloud-based assets, and allows us to make sure that we have a consistent set of policies between what we have onsite and what we have in the cloud. Having those things consistent gives us an added layer of security because we can ensure that things are going to be treated the same way, whether they're onsite or in the cloud. Authentication/single sign-on, as an example, credential mapping, device profiling, and also logging. All of those things should be consistent between both environments. That way we don't have discrepancies between the environments and perhaps miss something, thinking that we've configured it, but we only configured it on one side and not the other.

Application Security

Some other security considerations, application security - when we're designing these things, who can access the application? That sounds like a no brainer, but we have to make sure that we're not giving access to those who don't need it. Also, what dependencies exist and are those dependencies secured? Because it doesn't do us very much good to put a very expensive lock on the front door, but leave the back door wide open or a side window open, you get the idea. We have to make sure that all the interdependencies between applications are secured so we don't have a weak link in that chain. APIs, endpoints, single sign-on, we need to make sure all of these things are secured properly. Also, what technologies are used to defend against attacks, is it a cloud access security broker, is it a next gen secure web gateway, which we'll talk about in a moment, instance aware tools. We need to make sure that we're applying them consistently and that they're configured properly. Some of these tools have lots of bells and whistles and lots of knobs to turn, and if they're not configured, it gives us a false sense of security. It's very important that we apply consistent policies across the environment, but that we also understand what each of those policies do.

Next-gen Secure Web Gateway (NG-SWG)

Next-generation secure web gateways or next-gen SWGs. What this does is combine the features of multiple cybersecurity tools, such things as a cloud access security broker; DLP, or data loss prevention tools; activity controls, We can control at a very granular level who can do what and what specific activities they can and can't do; also instance-aware, we talked about being able to differentiate between corporate or personal or vendor or partner accounts and services, and then block or allow accordingly; and then some other things, like traditional secure web gateway functionality, API checking, policy enforcement, compliance enforcement, all those good things. All of those things combined make up a next-gen secure web gateway just understand what that tool is and the various features that it provides.

Firewall Considerations in a Cloud Environment

Next, let's talk about some firewall considerations in a cloud environment. Traditional firewalls performed IP filtering and packet inspection. They were able to identify threats at the perimeter, but they don't differentiate between corporate versions and personal versions of services. This is where instance-aware things come into play. Traditional firewalls did not address that. And then we have cloud-based apps, like Software as a Service, and

APIs introduce new challenges. Again, many more points that are publicly accessible, which means many more points that are, of course, targets for attack. Cloud access security brokers, also multi-cloud nuances. If you use each individual provider's firewall services, well, there's nuances between, so the configurations may not necessarily be consistent between environments. Also, multi-tenancy, that brings up different challenges as well simply because you have a lot of different groups that are utilizing the same infrastructure. Also, support, reskilling staff, change management, governance. All of these things come into play and, of course, should be a consideration when looking at firewall providers should you allow the cloud provider to also do on-prem firewall protection. All of these things should be thought about and considered when choosing firewall options, providers. There's a lot of nuances, there's no or wrong answer, and there's no one answer that's going to fit everybody. So, this is an area that will depend upon your specific organization. And then we also have DDOS, or distributed denial-of-service mitigation. Being able to detect in real time or close to real time and then scale as needed to be able to respond to different OSI layer attacks and then reroute traffic as necessary to reduce impact or drop it into a black hole? Then virtual firewalls, Firewall as a Service. These things enable granular segmentation? We talked about segmenting different areas, or micro-segmentation even, as needed around specific servers, applications, and services. You can segment at the subnet level, or you could scale down and get very granular and segment or firewall off at the actual application layer.

TCP/IP and OSI Models

The OSI model is a reference model designed to illustrate and standardize communication protocols, methods and devices. There's seven layers to the OSI model: application, presentation, session, transport, network, data-link, and physical. There's an OSI model, and then there's a TCP/IP model which breaks that into four layers instead of seven.

Application Layer, Protocol Layer, and Volumetric Attacks

If we have an attacker that's going to go ahead and create a botnet. They're going to infect a bunch of PCs out on the internet. And what they do with that botnet is send a bunch of HTTP GET requests to a web server, or to a target server. And in doing so, we're doing it at volume here with a bunch of hosts all sending these GET requests, and each time they do that, it spins up resources at the target. The attack is aimed at the OSI layer 7, for web servers. In a nutshell, the HTTP flood overwhelms the target system with requests that ends up exhausting resources on that target, and it takes it out of service. It makes it unable to service legitimate requests. Next, we have protocol attacks, and here we have the attacker with a bot, and what they're doing is aiming this at layer 3 and layer 4 of the OSI model, specifically targeting firewalls and load balancers. An attacker overwhelms the target with requests. In other words, they send the requests, the victim responds, but they never get the final confirmation from the attacker, so that just leaves it open. It never closes that connection, and it just exhausts resources. They send a bunch of SYN packets to the victim. The victim responds, but they never get the final confirmation. As that continues on and on, those requests build up. The victim or the target system just eventually runs out of resources. Next, we have volumetric attacks. Here we have an attacker, again, with his trusty bot and we have a bunch of DNS resolvers out on the internet. That attacker will use the bot or the botnet to send a bunch of requests over to DNS resolvers, but I have a fake or a spoofed IP address. The IP address will be that of the victim. That way, when a DNS server responds with the response, or the answer, to that request, they're sending it to the victim instead of to the bot. That goes over and over and over again. As the attacker spoofs DNS queries with the IP address of the victim, the DNS responses get sent to the target and eventually overwhelm, or consume, all of the target's bandwidth. They can't answer their own requests, they can't originate requests, and they get taken offline. They have no bandwidth left to do legitimate activities.

Cost

Costs are always a factor no matter what organization you're a part of, and at first glance, it usually appears that the cloud is cheaper than on-prem, and in many instances, it is, but like with everything within IT, there is a big old depends, in air quotes. If you spin up a bunch of resources, but you don't use them, its uptime, you have things up, you're not using them, you're still paying for them. If you do that same activity on an on-prem situation, you're not paying for that other than just the power, but you're not paying for all of the different sub pieces of that that you would be paying for in the cloud. Also, elastic expansion is great, but if you don't tear those things back down when you don't need them, costs continue to increase. Also, data ingress and egress depending upon the application, how much data goes in and out, you can be charged for all of that. Depending upon the application, depending upon what resources you have on-premise already, it could be cheaper, it just depends on the situation, how often you need it or how busy it is. Also CapEx versus

OpEx, that's an organizational preference. Some organizations are very CapEx friendly, some are very CapEx adverse. In other words, some would like to spend capital so they can depreciate the asset, all those like to do it as an OpEx, or an operational expense, so again it just depends upon your organization. There is no or wrong answer there.

Cloud Native Controls vs. Third-party Solutions
There are some nuances, and there are some pros and cons. With cloud-native controls, we have integration with the cloud provider. They are their native controls, so they work well across the board. To that point, security features are typically integrated with the other services that cloud provider offers. One potential downside, maybe, maybe not, is that the cloud provider, since it's their own tools, you and your team will need specific skills. A general set of skills typically don't apply because they're very specific to that cloud provider, and they may change from provider to provider, and also a bit of vendor lock in when you're looking at migrating or perhaps using multi-cloud environments. Then not necessarily always designed to be the most cost efficient. Not saying that they are, not saying that they're not, but they don't necessarily guide you along the way. There are services you can get, like well-architected solutions and things like that to make sure that you

are doing things in the most efficient way possible, but if you're doing it on your own, it's more of a self-service environment, you're not always going to necessarily design the most cost-efficient architecture, understanding when to take things up and down. With third-party solutions, you can manage similarly across clouds, so the same toolsets can be used no matter which cloud you're in, for the most part. Optimizations exist to reduce costs wherever possible, because they're not tied to a specific provider, so they try to make things as financially optimized as possible. And then additional security features around API access, privileges, secrets managements, you may have toolsets or features or functionality that don't exist with a cloud-native solution. It may or may not, depending upon the solutions that you choose. Then integration with other non-native applications, services, and automation. Third-party toolsets quite often are designed to work with a very wide range of tools of other third-party tools that aren't necessarily cloud native, so it gives you some options and potentially features that you wouldn't get in a cloud-native control or a cloud-native service. That doesn't apply all the time, of course. The cloud solutions are getting more and more full-featured every day. The big three come out with new services almost daily, so that becomes less and less of a distinction. And then tools typically work in a multi-cloud environment. If you're going to do all your work and you're never going to leave AWS or a Google Cloud platform or Azure, then great. If you're going to stay there forever, then that's not necessarily a concern. But if you do want to have a multi-cloud environment, maybe Cloud HA, the tools that you choose then become more critical. In this chapter, we covered a lot of great information dealing with cloud and cloud security, talking about cloud security controls, such things as high availability. Also, storage, network, and compute, the big three when it comes to the meat of any application or service. Also talked about various solutions like cloud access, security brokers, Secure Web Gateways, incidence aware. Then we talked about the pros and cons and the nuances between cloud-native controls and third-party toolsets.

Chapter 14 How to Implement Identity and Account Management Controls

In this chapter, we'll be covering implementing identity and account management controls. We have three main areas in this chapter. We have identity, we have account types, and then account policies. When it comes to identity, a few things to talk about. We have identity providers, or IdPs, and an identity provider stores and manages a user's identity. Something that which could be a username, or a password, or perhaps a PIN. Something that you have, which would be a badge or a smartphone. Then something that you are, a fingerprint, a retina scan, or some other type of biometric characteristic. This is used to authenticate users, otherwise known as principals, or other devices. It could be a laptop, a tablet, some other type of device. And then using two or more attributes to identify a user would be, as we know, multi-factor authentication. Depending upon the system that you're using, it may be that you only provide one of those three, or it could be multiples if it's a multi-factor authentication system. authentication factors, something that a password or some type of secret, something that you have, could be a smart card, could be a two-factor token, a PIN, or something that you are, like we talked about, a fingerprint, retina scan, some biometric characteristic. Then multi-factor authentication, two or more pieces of information used to authenticate, a PIN, a password, or a fingerprint. Also something to keep in mind is it must be from different categories. A password and a PIN, for instance, would only be one factor because both fall under something that you know. So for it to be multi-factor authentication, it should be from two different categories.

IdP Example

Here we have an IDP example, and we have Alice and she wants to access a ticketing application. Let's say it's a ticketing application for her work, and it is perhaps cloud based or uses an IDP or an identity provider. So she's going to attempt to access that application. It's going to realize that she's not currently signed on. What it does is it then goes out to an SSO provider or a single sign-on provider, and it will issue a request and say hey, can you let me in? Well, the single sign-on provider also realizes hey, she's not logged in. I can't authenticate her yet. It's going to prompt her to log into that application. It will then send her an SMS code, a username a password along with an SMS code, so it's going to be a two-factor authentication. Once Alice provides that information, it sends it back to the SSO provider who then will query an IDP. It'll issue what's called a SAML request to the IDP. A SAML request is a security assertion markup language, and it's a standardized way to tell external applications and services that a user is who they say they are. It doesn't authorize, but it authenticates. It sends that SAML request to the IDP. The IDP within authenticate, send that SAML response back to the SSO provider or the single sign-on provider who, in turn, then sends that SAML assertion back to the ticketing application and saying yes, Alice is who she says she is. Go ahead and let her log in to the application. When we're talking about attributes, an attribute is a piece of information about a user. It could be a username, an email address, a physical address. It could also be things like a company association, a role, a specific title, or contact info. There's many other things as well. These are just some examples of attributes, but these are what's contained potentially inside of an IDP record.

Certificates, Tokens, and SSH Keys

Digital certificates are electronic credentials that are issued to people, computers, and other electronic devices. Typically, people, or laptops, desktops, smart phones. They're used to authenticate and provide non-repudiation or to enable secure communications. It can also be applied in certain circumstances to IoT devices. Next, we have tokens. A token can have various uses, typically to authenticate an ID token, or to grant access to an API or some type of web application, which would in this case be called an access token. That's the two main types, ID tokens and access tokens, and we've talked about tokens in more depth in other chapters, so no need to dig in too deep here. And then we have SSH keys. They're used to securely authenticate when connecting to servers over SSH using a public key/private key certificate. As an example, if we are logged into Kali Linux, we have a terminal session opened, and from there you issue the command ssh-keygen, and that will generate a key that you can use to then connect securely to a remote system over SSH. If I open up that key file that was just generated, we see here's our private key, and then we can also take the corresponding public key, upload it to that server, and then use that to then securely communicate or connect with that session. Using tools like PuTTY or some other way to connect to a remote system, we can import that public key and then use it to securely connect and encrypt that communication to that remote server.

Certificate Issues

Certificate issues can result in people having access to a resource that they shouldn't have. If our certificates aren't correct, someone is able to have access to a rogue certificate or get one issued that they shouldn't have issued and they can have access potentially to resources they shouldn't have. Mechanisms need to be in place to quickly recall or replace a compromised certificate or a compromised certificate authority. We also need the ability to rotate keys and certificates and also keep track of how resources are secure. Keeping everything in a giant spreadsheet is not going to cut it, for a small environment, maybe, but at any type of scale, that's not going to be manageable. If that spreadsheet gets lost, if the keys get lost, if things aren't backed up, we could potentially lose access to those backups, or those resources, or whatever the case might be that we're talking about. We need to make sure we can secure that properly and also refer back to it when necessary. Many organizations don't have the infrastructure to quickly invalidate a compromised certificate. If a certificate authority within their network gets compromised, all the certificates that are issued by that certificate authority should also be recalled. If there is no infrastructure and no mechanism to do that, then you're potentially putting all those assets at risk. As an example, if you're not familiar with the certificate hierarchy, we start off with a root CA, a root certificate authority. Typically, we'll install that on our network. If we're going to self-serve our certificates, be our own CA, we would install that on our network, and then once everything is set up and configured, take that offline so that way it can't be compromised, we're taking the ability to have that root CA breached. We have a root CA that's offline, once it's configured, it will issue certificates to subordinate CAs. We'll also take those offline. this is for a large enterprise, we have disparate networks, we have maybe offices in different locations maybe in East Coast or West Coast, or maybe a global organization, the root CA that sits at the top of everything would issue certificates or subordinate CA certificates and all of those will be taken offline so that they're not compromised. From there, they would issue certificates to down-level CAs, the issuing CAs, those who remain online. That way when clients enroll in the network, they can contact that issuing CA and get a certificate for whatever it is they need a certificate for, accessing a resource, logging into the network, so on. Those things will stay online, but that way, if one of those issuing CAs is compromised, it's only for that small subset, it's not for the entire environment. If the subordinate CA or the root CA were compromised, then it's a much bigger deal, we want to make sure we break this up compartmentalize so we derisk the environment as much as possible. We also make it easier for our clients to get certificates. If someone on the West Coast is logging in, they don't want to necessarily have to contact the root CA, which may be in another part of the world. If we break this up in a hierarchy much like DNS or any other type of hierarchical system, we're attaching to a resource that's closest to where we are.

Smart Cards

Smart cards gives us access control, and it's also a security device. It contains a small chip, or an amount of memory on that card, and that card can contain information about us. It can be metadata about who we are, it could contain medical records, it could contain access, as far as like what doors we can access within a building, also, different levels of authorization or authentication for network resources. So, user permissions or access information. It's also typically combined with multi-factor authentication, such as a PIN or a password. One is something that you have, the other is something that you know. For it to be true two-factor authentication, it has to be from separate categories. We can set it up so that incorrectly entering a PIN or password X number of times can even shut that card down and render it invalid. That way, if it's stolen and someone's trying to just randomly brute force their way in, that will shut things down and not allow that to happen.

User Accounts

Under account types we have user accounts, the basic building block of our environment. User accounts are unique and are used for each person accessing a resource. It's a unique identifier that's assigned to each account. As let's say for instance in a Windows environment, we could have two users, there could be two users with the same exact name. But when I create the first account and the second account, they're going to have a unique ID or security identifier. In a Windows environment that's referred to as a SID. If I delete that account and then add it back again, well, the new account is a different SID. Even though the user account name might be the same, the security ID or the SID is going to be different. Every user should have their own account and be given the least amount of privileges required to do their work. It's known as a concept of least privilege. We don't want to give them more than they need, because that gives them the opportunity to then start exploring, perhaps delete things they shouldn't have access to, access things they shouldn't have access to, install malware, spyware or ransomware.

Account Management

Under account management, there are three main tenants that we want to be aware of. When dealing with shared and generic accounts and credentials, each user should have their own account, but even more importantly, each user should have their own non-admin account. Shared accounts are also too difficult to troubleshoot or audit in the event of a breach. Shared accounts are a no-no. Every user should have their own account, that account should be a non-admin account. That way, if that account is compromised, the person doing the compromising doesn't have that elevated privileges. But because typically, when ransomware, malware, or spyware is installed, it's installed in the context of the user account that installed it. If they're an admin, guess what? That malware or that spyware has admin privileges potentially. Next, when dealing with guest accounts. Guest accounts should be used sparingly if it all. Typically, best practices is to say, disable them. But, if for some reason we need to use them, use them sparingly. In kiosks or other public access locations, they may be acceptable or they may be required. The operating system should be reimaged frequently and locked down as much as possible in these environments. Typically in a kiosk environment, you may want to reimage that machine every day so that if someone goes out and installs software, malware, spyware, each day, well that just gets reimaged and you reduce and mitigate the likelihood that those things will permeate through the system. Next, when dealing with service accounts, service accounts should only be used for, not surprisingly enough, services, not for users, and they should also be unique for each service. That way you can quickly identify what service account is accessing which service or is representing which service. Troubleshooting, audits, and revoking permissions becomes much easier when we understand what that service account impacts. If we use one service account and we give that to everything, 5 applications, 10 applications, and then we need to disable that for some reason, well, we've just disabled potentially 5 or 10, 15, 20 apps, however many we have assigned to that. It makes it very, very difficult to troubleshoot.

Password Complexity
Passwords should be complex enough to be hard to guess, that's a no brainer; however, they shouldn't be so long or so complex that our users need to write them down. That's the key differentiator here, and I think there's a fine line between usability and security. We want to make them secure enough so they can't be brute forced or easily guessed, but not Much that we have to have them written down to remember them. Passphrases often are easier to remember. Instead of having an eight character password, you might have a complete sentence or maybe a couple words in a sentence, but if it's something that's easy for that person to remember, a sentence, it's long enough to become very difficult to guess, but still easy enough for them to remember without having to write things down. Just something to keep in mind that might work in

your environment. Also, we can enforce the minimum length. We have to have a password be at least six characters or at least eight characters, or whatever is appropriate for your environment. With policy, we can enforce those types of restrictions. We can also say you have to have a special character, whether it is an asterisk or an exclamation point, parentheses and so on. By having special characters, again, we're making things more difficult to guess. Also, upper/lowercase. We might mandate that the password contain at least one uppercase letter just to make things more difficult for someone to try to guess or brute force.

Password History

All of these things are used in conjunction with one another to limit or mitigate the risk of someone trying to brute force or guess someone's password. Password history, that's going to dictate how many passwords are remembered by the OS before a user is allowed to reuse a password if they ever are. The minimum amount of time before a user can change passwords is also very helpful. And if we use these two things in conjunction with one another, we have a very secure policy. And how that works is that okay you have to go through, let's say, 5 or 10 passwords before you can reuse that password again. Let's just say I like the password. P@sswOrd1.

Well, when it comes time to change, what do users typically do? it's P@sswOrd2. Comes time to change again, P@sswOrd3. And they'll cycle through until they get back to what they like, which might be P@sswOrd1. If we have a 10-password reuse cycle, they have to go through 10 passwords before they can get back to P@sswOrd1. Well, sometimes if we don't have this minimum amount of time in place, users are a little wise, and they'll sit there and they'll change your password over and over and over and over again. They'll cycle through those 10 different passwords so they can get back to P@sswOrd1, which is the one they like and that's the one they remember. That's a no-no. That defeats the whole password history and the changing your password option. By putting the minimum amount of time that a user must maintain that password before they can change it, we mitigate that risk. If we make it say you have to have that password for two days before you can change it again. They change it to pass from P@sswOrd1 to P@sswOrd2. They try to change it to P@sswOrd3 away, no good. It's going to say no, you have to wait 2 days before you can change to P@sswOrd3. That might be frustrating to them a little bit, but from the company's perspective, much more secure. It prevents that getting around the password history requirement.

Password Reuse

We can define via policy whether the user can even ever use the same password again. If you say no, once you use the password, you can never use it again, you might have a mutiny on your hands, that could be problematic for some users, but a password history of 15, 20 might be even a little bit excessive, but it certainly is doable and much more workable than saying once you use it once, you can never use it again. I wouldn't necessarily recommend that policy, but we can do all of those things of policy and enforce that across the enterprise. It can be used in conjunction with the password history. We can say it'd have to go through X number of passwords before they can, in fact, reuse that password. Next is password length. We want to make sure we define a minimum number of characters and why do we do that? Well, we don't want it to make easy to guess. We don't want the password to be one or two or A or B, we want them to have a minimum number of characters. Most secure passwords are six to eight characters in length, it can be used in conjunction with complexity requirements to ensure that users have to use uppercase, lowercase, or some type of special character, asterisk, exclamation point, and so on.

Time of Day Restrictions

Another one that may or may not be appropriate for your environment, or every environment, is different, but is time of day restrictions. What this does, it will limit a user's access to files, folders, servers, or the entire network, depending upon the time of day. What it does is it keeps users who have no need to access corporate resources after hours, or from a certain set of hours, from accessing, poking around, and potentially getting access to sensitive company information. It keeps them from having additional opportunities to exfiltrate data. By limiting a user's access to just before and just after normal working hours, you limit that exposure risk by roughly 16 hours a day. That may or may not be appropriate for your environment. As we know, in IT, there are typically people on standby around the clock, depending upon the type of industry in your environment. It may not be applicable, but if so, if it makes sense, then consider time of day restrictions. That way you can ensure those users who have no need to be in your network don't have access.

User Access Best Practices

When it comes to user access best practices, three things I want to talk about account maintenance. We need to automatically disable temporary accounts after a period of time, periodically audit to ensure group memberships are appropriate as well.

What do I mean by that? Well, when contractors come on board, typically, it's going to be for a finite period of time, whether that's a month, 3 months, 6 months. While the day that account is created, we should have an auto expire after some period of time, let's just say 6 months. If we need to extend that, we could have an automated process in place where the manager gets an email says, hey, this account is about to expire, do want to extend it. Reply yes or no, and if yes, then that automated process will extend that account for another 6 months or they may log into a portal and just click on that user account and say extend, but by doing that every 6 months or whatever that period of time is, it ensures that we don't forget about it and ensures that that user account, that contractor account that was created, 5 years ago isn't still active because if it's an account that no one is accessing, then if a hacker continuously tries to get into that account and locks it out every so often why no one is going to notice because no one is trying to use the account. It's very good, best practice in fact, for us to automatically disable those temporary accounts after a period of time. Also ensure group membership doesn't change without our knowledge. Next, we have group-based access control, again important that we assign permissions to groups and not individual users. Well, why is that? Because when we start to assign to individual users, it becomes a nightmare to try to troubleshoot. If a user is a member of five different groups and we know what all those different groups' permissions are, but they still can't access a resource or they're still having some type of trouble, well, then come to find out they have a different level of access assigned to their individual user account, it can conflict potentially with what's assigned at the group level. As an example, if they have deny assigned, they could be a member of five different groups that have full control to a resource, but if they have individually been assigned no access, well that's going to trump everything else. The effective permission is no access, so always assign permissions at the group level. Then location-based policies. As users move from place to place, we need to ensure permissions and access adjust accordingly. Because, we don't want to assign more access and more privileges than the user needs? Always keep that concept in mind of least privilege. If you can always remember that, it's going to go a long way to ensuring users don't have more than they need and it will help mitigate that risk overall.

Permissions Auditing and Review
When it comes to permissions, auditing and reviewing, permissions are not a set it and forget it thing. I had that in quotes. It's not something we

should do once and then never look at again. Periodic audits are going to ensure permissions are intact and also still appropriate. What do I mean by that? Well, as a person changes jobs, from time to time, and are given more responsibility, less responsibility, they may change roles, go to different departments, their permissions are going to change as well. As they go to a new role and they get new permissions, new access to different things, we need to make sure we're removing the old ones, the access to the old things. That way they don't start to accumulate things over time. They've been at a company for 20 years, all of a sudden they have access to everything because they've been gathering along the way. It's important to make sure that we have policies in place, automated, if possible, so as they change roles, their group membership will automatically dictate what they do or do not have access to. By periodically reviewing and auditing as well, it's going to give us the opportunity to ensure that additional s haven't been granted or changed without permission. At some point in time, someone gave someone s they shouldn't have had access to, or they may have gotten something temporarily and it was never taken away. By periodically auditing these things, we can ensure people have just what they need to do their work and no more, getting back to that concept of least privilege.

Recertification

Credentials and required clearances need to be audited and periodically recertified, whether that's every 6 months, once a year, once a quarter, floor certified individuals coming into your data center, technicians working on pieces of equipment or having access to resources hardware, software, or data. Levels of access and also the locations being accessed should be periodically audited and they should be recertified because as a company grows over time or they deal with different contractors, different vendors, the vendors themselves will shift personnel around from time to time, well, if that person that was accessing our data center 6 months ago has moved on to another position, or perhaps even another company, we need to make sure we revoke that person's access because if it's left there, guess what, that's an account that potentially is not being monitored, something that a hacker can then use and bang against if he gets locked out every so often, no one cares because no one is trying to use it so no one sees that it's locked out, and then when the lockout resets itself, the hacker can try again and he has the opportunity to potentially bruteforce those accounts, Disable the accounts and revoke access as soon as that is no longer needed. Also, when we deal with equipment or infrastructure, when infrastructure is refreshed where application is updated, we should recertify them again, make sure that the connections, the security protocols, the firewall changes that are in place are still applicable. Do we need more or do we need less? If something changes, an application changes, and it used to use 10 different ports and the updated version of that only uses 1 port, well, there is an opportunity to reduce or mitigate our risk by removing those 9 ports, by closing those 9 holes in our firewall. Periodically, auditing and recertifying infrastructure and applications is definitely a good practice.

Group Policy

Within a Windows environment, we can use group policy to enforce password rules. We can use it to enforce such things as complexity, meaning a user has to enter a password that is, meets certain criteria whether it's a minimum number of characters, it could be uppercase/lowercase, it could have special characters like an exclamation point or parentheses. We can also say, when does that password expire? Is it every X number of 30 days, 45 days, 6 months? If we have contractors, we can set up an automated process that says, every six months that account will expire unless it's automated to extend. Certain environments might say, contractor comes in, you automatically get six months of access, or shorter if you need it, but six months max. Then if the actual company needs to extend that, maybe the person who hired that contractor might get an automated email that says, password is about to expire. Do you want to extend that? And in a lot of instances, the actual employee or the hiring manager might just simply say approve or just send back an email, that'll kick that workflow off and extend that contractor's account for another six months. But it's a good practice so that things don't extend out further than they need to. We can also enforce group membership via group policy, say who belongs to what groups, and we can also make sure that users don't try to sneak themselves into privileged groups like administrators. It can automatically run and say, these users need to be in this group, let's say the admin's group or domain admin group; or whatever we define as a special group or a privileged group, and if so and so sneaks in the back door, well every 30 minutes or so that's going to rerun through that policy and say, wait a minute, you don't belong in here, and pull him out. That makes sure that we increase our security footprint as much as possible or strengthen that position I should say, so that people don't slip in and try to go in unnoticed. We can also set things like remote access time of day, and then the length of a connection. In other words, let's just say people can remotely access our systems, but if it's after 6 PM, so that shrinks our exposure window by 12 hours. For a 24/7 shop, that's probably not the best policy.

And we can also say once you log in, you can only stay connected for an hour, two hours, six hours. By limiting how long they can stay connected, again, we reduce the amount of damage someone could do if they're in here trying to do something harmful to the company.

Expiration

The next thing is password or account expiration. Temporary accounts should have an expiration date set when they are created. The reason I say that is because as an administrator, if we are in a relatively large or very large environment, we're not going to remember to disable that account we created 3 weeks ago, or a month ago, or 6 months ago, just too many of them to manage. If we do that in an automated fashion, and say, every user account that we create, if it's a temporary or a contractor account, as an example, we're going to give them 30 days, or maybe 3 months, or 6 months of access. At that point, it automatically disables unless we extend. There are a number of systems out there, and again it's going to depend on your environment, but there are a number of things that we can due to plug into your directory management or your account management system that will say, 15 days, or maybe, 3 weeks before that account is set to expire, we'll start emailing the account creator, or the hiring manager, and say, this is getting ready to expire, if you want to extend this, just reply back to this email, or log into this website, or send an email to the, the AD, or the directory service administrator, somethings are more automated than others, but by doing that, we automatically guarantee or build in the fact that user accounts, temporary accounts, contractor accounts are not going to extend beyond their useful life That way, after a couple of years, we have 30, 40, 50, 100 temporary accounts that people are long gone, but those accounts are still active, those things become security risks, they are things that are not monitored. It's an attack surface for a hacker, and they have an account that they can bang against and try to brute force or do whatever with it that no one's monitoring, those are all risks that, as security professionals, we need to mitigate. It ensures that administrators don't forget to disable and expire accounts, we covered that. We leave accounts intact, just disabled, that's the differentiator. We don't want to necessarily delete that account, we want to just disable it. It can always be enabled later because if we delete that account, we also delete the security ID, or the SID, associated with that account. If there are encrypted files or things that we need that are specific to that exact account, if we delete it, even if we, even if we recreate with the same username, that SID is different. In effect, from the computer's perspective or from the OS' perspective, it's a different account. So, we can also, extend that account through some type of automated method, so there's no way or wrong way to do that, but just the main take away is we want to automatically or pre-configure that expiration to take place at X amount of days after that account is created.

Recovery

Can users recover their own passwords? Some environments, that's applicable, some it's not. It just depends upon your environment. However, if you have a password recovery process, let's make sure that security questions aren't easily discovered. We want to make sure that they don't put in like their kids names, pets names or favorite vacation spots, so these types of things are more of a training issue than an automated issue, but we need to make sure that users are very well versed in this because as a skilled social engineer and if I realize that most people are going to use their dog's name or their children's name, their favorite car, vacation spot, sports figure, there are a handful of things that most people will use as a password if given the choice. If I sit down and have a conversation with someone, I strike up a conversation at the water cooler or in the break room and say, hey, where you guys going for vacation this week or it's an awesome a picture of your kids I saw on your on your on your desk, what are their names, or I love your dog, what's his name? When you spend five minutes and just have a conversation with someone, you can get very valuable pieces of information that you can then use to try to guess bruteforce people's passwords, so those types of things should be educated into users in the back of their mind, don't use these things as passwords, or if you're going to do that or if they do it, make sure they replace those characters with special characters and enforce a uppercase lowercase policy. And then policy will define if users need to call the help desk or if they have self-service options, maybe some type of call-in or IVR System, or a web portal they can visit, or they may have to just wait 15, 20 minutes, 30 minutes for that account to unlock itself.

Impossible Travel/Risky Login
Impossible travel or risky login is a security feature many cloud-based applications have, and you may even have it internal to your organization, but in this instance, it will utilize AI and ML, or artificial intelligence and machine learning, to determine what's normal and also what's risky. Logins from IP addresses or locations within a timeframe that is shorter than the expected travel time, as an example, that requires an initial learning period typically like a week or so to understand what's normal and what's

not normal, but it allows you to programmatically understand what should be a normal log in. For instance, if someone logs in from the East Coast and then 20 minutes later, they log in from the West Coast well, unless they've developed some type of time portal, and if they did, I don't know why they'd use it the log in from one coast to the other, I'd probably use it for some other purpose, but let's say they did, well then, of course, that would be normal, but assuming they don't have a time travel portal or can't travel faster than the speed of light, then that would be an unusual login., of course, they could use a VPN and log in from different locations, but that would also be part of the learning process. During that learning period, we may learn that user A logs in from a VPN periodically depending upon what they're doing, so that may eventually not get flagged as unusual, but for the most part, that would be flagged as a risky or an impossible travel login. And as an example, if we look at Azure cloud security portal ready for this specific instance, we see there are some alerts generated impossible travel activity for a specific user or a specific service? We flag that and then issue alerts to the administrator and say, hey, there is something suspicious going on, this user logged in what we're flagging as impossible travel or risky log in, here is the information, here are the details, and then the administrator could then take further action, if necessary. There are a number of ways to do this, we could do it manually or programmatically through this cloud app security, as an example, but it's not the only way to do it, but just understand the concept of an impossible travel or a risky log in. We're trying to flag activity for users that would just not be able to do what it is they're doing. It could be indicative of someone trying to hacking account, if someone logged in from the East Coast and then a half hour later or 10 minutes later, they logged in from another country, they couldn't possibly travel that far, well it could be, it could be normal activity via VPN, or it could be someone hacking that account from another country that's trying to get in to that account, so it definitely warrants some additional investigation.

Lockout

A policy should be put in place that automatically locks a user's account after "X" number of times that they incorrectly log into the system or try to log into the system. Typically it's 3-5. You can adjust that up or down, depending upon your environment. But, once an account is locked out, it will typically stay locked out for 20-30 minutes or maybe upwards of an hour. But the key thing here is we want to make that lockout duration long enough to thwart brute force attacks. A 30 minute period is usually good. That way a user can't just continuously run a script or sit there at a keyboard and trying to bang away one after the other after the other, trying to get information or trying to guess a user's password. It will lock out after three attempts or five attempts. Then they have to wait a half an hour.

Disablement

That brings me to disablement, and I talked about this briefly before, but we should disable unused accounts instead of deleting them. And we have already covered the fact that a user account has a security ID, or a SID, under the hood? We look at the user account as lowest X, or lowest one, or lowest two, or whatever, but under the hood, it's some long string of characters alphanumeric numbers that is the security ID. That's what the computer recognizes as that account. If we delete them, they can have a different SID, even if we recreate them with the same username. If that user encrypted documents or did some things that are specific to that user account and then we delete them, we're going to have a much harder time trying to recover that information. Instead of deleting, let's just disable. Once we do that, we can always re-enable it later. In this chapter, we covered three main areas. We talked about identity and all the things associated with a user account, IDPs, attributes, multi-factor authentication. We also talked about various account types and we talked about account policies like lockouts, disablements, impossible travel, risky logins, and various ways to make sure that our accounts are secure as possible.

Chapter 15 How to Implement Authentication and Authorization Solutions

In this chapter, we'll be covering implementing authentication and authorization solutions. We have three main areas again. We have authentication management, talking about passwords, trusted platform chapters, hardware security methods. Some of these terms should be familiar to you. Also authentication methods, talking about protocols and platforms that we use to authenticate users in the environment. And then access control schemes, talking about security settings and methods. When we're talking about authentication management, there's some concepts that you should be familiar with; password keys. We're talking about public key or private key, or it could even be a master key to key vaults. You should be familiar with both PKI infrastructure, public key/private key, and also using them whenever possible, whether it's for SSH connections to servers, whether it is certificate management for various connectivity for communication, transfer of files, or connecting to remote servers, and our master keys to key vaults. And when I say a key vault, I mean a password vault. A secure platform that enables you to store passwords for either automated retrieval or manual retrieval. You can place passwords in this vault to allow users to access them so they don't have to keep them somewhere where hackers or attackers could get access to them easily. A password vault would be a secure area on the network, typically a platform like CyberArk or KeePass as an example. Some are more enterprise ready than others. But you can place your passwords in there and either use them just as a dumping ground, where you have to go in and manually retrieve them, or some of the more full-feature platforms are API enabled Your applications and programs can programmatically access those vaults, the API, and use the passwords within there without having to extract or type those things in manually. Some can also rotate passwords on a predefined schedule, again, removing some of that manual user intervention from the process. Then we've talked before about the Trusted Platform Chapter, or TPM chip, which is a secure area usually embedded on a device, whether it be a laptop, a server, perhaps even a smartphone, they have secure areas within those devices as well, so that's where we can store cryptographic keys to keep them out of prying eyes. Then we have hardware security chapters, or HSMs, and this is similar in form and function to a TPM chip; however, this is on a card that can be inserted into a server and also be used to securely store cryptographic keys. Then we have knowledge-based authentication, otherwise known as a secret question. It's a component of MFA, or multi-factor authentication. In this case, a user's asked a secret question, perhaps what's your favorite dog's name, or where'd you go to high school, or what was your first place that you held a job? These things are good to an extent. Keep in mind if you do use knowledge-based authentication and you have common questions like this, a lot of things out there on social platforms are geared towards getting the answers to these questions. You'll notice on some of the social media platforms they have quizzes and little games you can get into where they'll ask you your high school mascot or test your knowledge about the first place you worked. Well, those things could conceivably be used to gather information that could then be paired with user identities down the road. If they're able to get this information and then pair this up with usernames or passwords that is either stolen from that person or that application directly or combined with other breaches, that can give a lot of information that can answer some of these secret questions. If you have the ability to set up secret questions within your organization, make them such that they're not easily guessable or something that a social engineer would be able to pull from someone just by asking a few innocuous, or at least seemingly innocuous, questions.

Extensible Authentication Protocol (EAP)

EAP, or Extensible Authentication Protocol was defined by RFC 3748 and then replaced by RFC 5247. It's an authentication framework, as opposed to a specific authentication mechanism, but EAP is widely in use across a number of different formats, roughly 40 different formats currently, and some of which you may be familiar with, such things as LEAP, EAP-TLS, or EAP-IKEv2. The takeaway being that an Extensible Authentication Protocol, extensible, meaning it can be added to, you can plug things into it. It gives us a framework that other things can use, whether it's TLS or other authentication mechanisms, perhaps that haven't even been invented yet, but it gives that framework that these things can then plug into very easily.

Challenge Handshake Authentication Protocol (CHAP)

Next, we have something referred to as CHAP, and CHAP stands for challenge handshake authentication protocol. CHAP was originally used to authenticate PPP clients, or point to point protocol clients, to a server, clients dialing in or accessing a remote server. It's a one-way hash based on a shared secret, in this case, a user's password is compared at both the client and the server. Plain text is never sent over the wire, and as an example, we have a client that wants to log into a server. When that client connects to that resource, the server will turn back and say enter your password. The client does not enter or send the password in clear text over the wire. What it does is it runs a challenge handshake authentication protocol, or CHAP, it hashes the user's password, and then passes the hash over the wire. The server on the other side knows that user's password has it in its database, it's going to run that same hashing algorithm against the password. If the hashes match, then the client is given access to that resource.

Password Authentication Protocol (PAP)
Next, we have something referred to as PAP, or Password Authentication Protocol. This has been deprecated. It's a username and password that's sent in plain text. With a username and password being sent in clear text, it's easy to see why that's no longer used. Again, as an example, we have the client and the server. The client's going to send their full username and password in clear text. Anyone with any type of packet sniffer can pull that information off the wire. What's happening is the user sends their username and their password in clear text, the server's going to check that against its database and then grant or deny access. But as we know, as security professionals, that's a bad idea. Sending things in clear text, very easy to pull

that information off the wire using Wireshark or some other type of protocol analyzer or network sniffer. We don't use this specific authentication protocol anymore.

Port Security and 802.1x Authentication
The next concept I want to talk about is port security and 802.1x, securing physical access to the network. We want to control the ability of someone to just walk into our environment, whether it be a kiosk at a retail store, or a library, or a school, or even within our corporate environment, we don't want to necessarily have someone being able to walk up, pull out their laptop, pull out a CAT5 cable, plug it into the wall, and gain access to our network. One way we can do that is through something called port security. This is particularly applicable to things like kiosks, schools, libraries, not necessarily throughout an entire environment, it becomes a little bit unwieldy at that point, but for specialized situations where we want to control specific access to specific ports, port security is definitely a good fit there. What we can do is configure a switch so that it only learns one MAC address per port. We can keep attackers from sending multiple fake addresses. So, in other words, someone can't pull out their laptop, plug in, and then just start bombarding our network with fake MAC addresses. Because if you recall, when we have our devices and

it connects to a switch, that very first time it does that, it goes out and tries to get an IP address via DHCP, or it may have one hard-coded, it's going to try to ARP for some resources, it might go to DNS, it might go to whatever the case might be, try to resolve a URL, whatever action is taking place, it's going to put datagrams onto the network. As soon as it does that, the MAC address of that device is attached to that datagram. It's a layer 2 piece of information. The switch, which is a layer 2 device, will learn, or memorize, that MAC address and associate it with that port. And so the switch will learn over time all of the devices that are connected to it, what MAC addresses are associated with which ports, so that way, when information comes in, it knows what port to send that information out of. It's a very directed process. Broadcasts will go out all ports, but if it's traffic between PC1 and PC2, PC1 is connected to the port 1, PC2 is connected to the port 10, as an example, it will only go in port 1 and out port 10. So that keeps things more secure. However, as I was mentioning, we have malicious individuals or malicious activity that can take place where someone could flood a specific port and overrun the MAC table on that switch and bring it down. By sending port security and only allowing certain MAC addresses or one MAC address per port, we negate that ability for someone to do that type of activity. We can also use that in conjunction with something called 802.1x to strengthen security at the wall jack. As I mentioned before with, school setting as an example, or a kiosk, we have something called 802.1x authentication. What that is, is EAPOL, or Extensible Authentication Access Protocol, over LAN, over a local area network. That Extensible Authentication Access Protocol gives us the ability to say, when somebody connects to our wall jack, we're not going to allow them to communicate until they authenticate with the network. They're going to authenticate with something called a RADIUS server. It's an authentication server. In this schema, it's a multi-part process, the client, which is in the terms of this authentication process, is called a supplicant, the client is going to initiate a request that they're going to plug into the wall jack, they're going to say, hey, can I communicate? The switch is going to say no, not until you authenticate. It will only allow EAPOL traffic to pass through that port, it will send it off to the authentication server, all of these things have to be configured in place so that this process takes place, but once it's set up, the port will not be activated until that authentication process is complete. The supplicant will send information to the switch, the switch will then forward it onto the authentication server. Once the credentials are validated and verified, in other words, the client is authenticated, and then the authentication server sends that information back and says, yes, you can communicate, the port is wide open, and of course, the supplicant or the client can communicate on the network.

RADIUS
We have something we refer to as RADIUS, and that stands for Remote Authentication and Dial-in User Service. It started out as Remote Authentication and Dial-In User Service, but people are coming in from cable, from fiber, from other mechanisms, so it's not just referring to dial in, but the concept is the same. It provides AAA capabilities. When I say AAA, I mean three things. It provides authentication, and authentication identifies the user and allows or denies access. We're going to identify that user and either allow them or deny them access. We can also challenge for additional credentials, a two-factor authentication, such as a PIN or a rotating code. They may have a key fob or a dongle. Then next, it's going to provide for authorization, and that deals with providing things like the length of time allowed on the network, access control lists, or ACLs, for various resources, and then on top of that, we're going to provide accounting. Accounting is used for tracking the start and stop time of each session, and it can be used for billing, or perhaps showback, to show how long the user was connected to that service. If we look at an example, we have Alice and

she's referred to as a supplicant. We're talking about a RADIUS example where we have a supplicant, we have an authenticator, and then an authentication server, or AS. And you'll also see an AD or LDAP server off in the distance here. That is the actual mechanism that's going to pull up the user account and make sure that they're in the system. Alice perhaps wants to access a resource. She wants to connect to a wireless access point in this example. Well, rather than have each individual wireless access point have her username and credentials, there may be dozens within her environment, they simply are configured to point to a RADIUS server. That way, Alice goes to log in, the supplement to the authenticator. The authenticator is simply going to pass through that request to the RADIUS server. The RADIUS server is what provides the authentication. The RADIUS server's going to contact AD or LDAP, depending on how it's configured, and say, does Alice exist, and what are her credentials? Is she allowed access or not? And if so, we'll reply back positively, replies back to the wireless access point, and she's allowed access. We can further go on, and if we wanted to layer on 802.1X authentication, we can also make sure that Alice's machine can log into that wireless access point as well. We can not just necessarily filter by MAC address or by IP address, we can also filter by account credentials as well. There has to be a valid account on the network before authentication is granted to that wireless access point.

Single Sign-on (SSO)

Next up is single sign-on and single sign-on is a method of allowing users to access all resources that they're going to need, within an environment with a single username and a password. It negates having to remember multiple usernames and passwords. We talked about previously, whether it be a Kerberos realm or Active Directory or some other authentication mechanism or directory service, by having that in place, a user can sign on once to a directory server or an Active Directory server and some type of directory service and then access everything within that environment. Of course, they have to have access granted to them? They can't just login and automatically access everything. Each individual resource is still controlled by ACLs, but they don't need to remember username and passwords for each resource, so it makes it much more secure, mitigates risk by keeping users from having to write down credentials. If you have to remember, 50 different passwords or 100 different passwords for your work environment, it's going to be very difficult to keep those straight in your head, you're going to have to start writing those things down. Once they're written down, make the task much easier for a hacker to come in and retrieve that information, not to mention the fact that come password changing day, it's a lot easier to change your password once and have it propagate everywhere or have access everywhere rather than having to remember to change your password on 50 different resources or 100 different resources, whatever your environment entails by having to do that each and every time become a very tedious process.

SAML

SAML stands for the Security Association Markup Language, and what this is authenticating through a third-party to gain access to some resource. That resource being accessed isn't responsible for the authentication. You may see this a lot when you're browsing websites out on the Internet, you may go to a website and it asks you to log in, but you're not going to login on that site specifically, you might log in with your Google ID, or an email address, or some type of open ID, or your Facebook account, or your Twitter account. These different things can act as a trusted third-party that will pass through to the site you're trying to access. The authentication requests are passed to that trusted third-party server, the user authenticates to the third-party server, they're issued a token, that token is passed to the target resource. We have a client, we have a resource server that we're trying to get to, and then we have some AS server, the authentication service so that's going to be SAML, in this case. If we look at an example, we have a client, the resource server, and the AS server. The user wants to access a URL, they want to go out to a resource. Well, what's going to happen is that resource server will post to the AS, with an authorization request to the SAML server. If that user is not already logged in, then they're going to be asked to log in, they're going to log into that AS server, or the SAML server, because there is a good chance you may already be logged into one of these third-party services, and you may be logged into Twitter or Facebook or whatever ahead of time. When that happens, you're redirected to the resource that you're trying to get to with the SAML token and you're logged into that resource server represented with the web page or the resource that you're trying to get to. There are some SAML alternatives. The federated ID concept has several methods that are currently in use. SAML is not the only one. SAML is one that we mentioned, but then we have also OpenID and also OAuth, so they all provide similar features and functionality. However, many of the most popular websites function as the trusted third-party, they use either OAuth or open ID. If you log into a website using your Facebook credentials or your Google ID or your Twitter account, you're using one of those too, probably not SAML, but the concept is the same. I just want to make sure you understand the concept and how it's passed from that trusted third-party onto the site that you're accessing.

TACACS

TACACS stands for terminal access controller access-control system. TACACS was originally developed in 1984 for controlling access to MILNET - the military network. TACACS is not in use anymore, it's been replaced by newer versions, but I just want to give you an idea of where things have come from and where we're at currently. TACACS has been replaced by something called XTACACS, Extended terminal access controller access-control system. This was a proprietary set of extensions to TACACS developed by Cisco in 1990. It added those three additional features that we talked about previously authentication, authorization, and accounting. RADIUS had it, TACACS, at that point, did not. However, the takeaway here is that XTACACS is not backwards compatible with TACACS. We added three things, authentication, authorization, and accounting, and then no backwards compatibility with TACACS.

TACACS+

Next we have TACACS+. This is the most common implementation of TACACS, which is why I wanted to focus in this area, just give you an idea of where we've come from with the other two previous versions. TACACS+ is the most common implementation, it's going to run on TCP over port 49. It also encrypts the entire communication, so that's something new for TACACS+. Previously, it only encrypted the very beginning piece. We encrypt the entire communication, much more secure. It's not vulnerable to the security issues associated with radius. Some key differentiations and I'm going to compare and contrast those two here in just a moment, but remember that, not vulnerable to security issues because it encrypts the entire communication, and it also separates authentication and authorization to allow more granular control. We can split those out to separate servers, so we don't necessarily have to have everything running on one server. As with the previous version, it's not backward compatible with its predecessors. If we look at RADIUS versus TACACs+, there are a couple things we should be aware of. With RADIUS, it combines authentication and authorization, it encrypts only the password, requires each network device to contain authorization configuration, there is no command logging, minimal vendor support for authorization, UDP, which is connectionless, and, of course, the UDP port set operates upon 1645 and 46, 1812 and 13. It's designed for subscriber AAA, not necessarily for administrator or administration. TACACS+, on the other hand, separates all three elements of AAA making it more flexible, it's also going encrypt the username and the password. That's very important to understand. It also allows for centralized management of authorization and configuration, so that's going to give us a lot more flexibility and allow it to scale on a much larger sense. It has full command login as well and it's also supported by most major vendors. It's TCP oriented, which is connection oriented? UDP is connectionless, TCP is connection oriented, it operates off of TCP port 49, and it's designed for administrator AAA.

oAUTH

OAuth is an open standard for authorization. It's commonly used as a way for internet users to log into third-party websites using their accounts at some of the big providers - Google, Facebook, Microsoft and Twitter. But, it allows them to do without exposing their individual password. They can log in or use the login credentials from those bigger services, that's a trusted third-party, and then when you access whatever resource it is you're going to access, they query Google or they query Facebook, and make sure that you are who you say you are and you have the proper authorization. It allows access tokens to be issued to that third-party client by an authorization server with the approval of the resource owner. It's all tied in. As an example, you have a user that wants to access some client applications. They're going to request a service, they're redirected back to the authorization server, and then there's an authorization between user and authorization server, that authorization is granted. They're redirected with that authorization code. It then requests a token with that authorization code, which goes back to the client application. It goes all the way out to the actual resource server, which comes back to the client application, response is sent back to the user, the user requests the service, request for the data with the access token is sent to the resource server, and then it's sent back to the client application and then back to the user. All of this happens behind the scenes, so all you do is click on a resource, you sign in with your Google or Facebook or whatever, Twitter account, that authorization takes place. All of this happens behind the scenes, you don't even see any of this, and all you know is you log into that resource. So, just understand that there are some things taking place under the covers, and that you need to know the basics of the process. However, you don't have control over how Google or Twitter or Facebook mandates their process. Just understand that they're a trusted third-party, and that authentication is used to authenticate to other external resources.

OpenID and Shibboleth

OpenID is a standard, it's an open standard that provides SSO capabilities. The cooperating sites that participate in this OpenID framework, they're called relying parties or RP. A user chooses an OpenID provider, and there are a number, and they use that account to log into any website that accepts OpenID authentication. I'm sure you've seen this before where you go to a website, and it may give you the option of creating an account or logging in with your email address. Or you can log in with your Facebook credentials, Google account, Twitter. It gives you that ability to log in with a trusted third-party ID. And then we have something referred to as Shibboleth, and that's based on SAML, we talked about previously. It provides a free and open source federated single sign-on and attribute exchange framework. It's similar to OpenID in concept. Shibboleth also provides extended privacy functionality, which allows a user and their home site to control the attributes released to each application. You have some finegrain control over what is shared. When you log on it may be configured to just send perhaps your username and email address, or it could send additional attributes as well, whatever is configured within that framework, to share between entities.

Kerberos

Kerberos is, in Greek mythology, a three-headed dog that guarded the gates of Hades, and its applicable here because there's three components when a user or a client wants to access some type of service. It's a network authentication service that was originally developed by MIT, and is used for mutual authentication between client and server. This gives us that dual authentication I talked about before where the client authenticates to the server, the server also authenticates to the client. Some key terminology before we get into the details here. We have something referred to as a KDC, or a key distribution center; we have an authentication service, or the AS; we have a ticket-granting ticket; we have a ticket-granting service; a principal; and an authenticator. If we look at this in a little more detail, I'm just going to cover this at more or less a high level. You don't need to dig down into the nitty-gritty details for the exam, but just for your own information, there are a couple of things that go on here in the background. The client wants to connect to a service. The client needs to authenticate, we're using KDC, or a key distribution center, which in a Windows environment is going to be the domain controller. That's going to contain the authentication service, and also the ticket-granting service to give those TGTs. The client will send that request to the KDC, or the authentication service, the authentication service will generate what's called a session key. It's going to encrypt that session key with the user's password and it encrypts the session key and this user's username, which is also referred to as a Kerberos principal. It's going to create what's called a service ticket and send that back to the client. There's two pieces to that. The client can decrypt the first part, because it has its password. The password, incidentally, is not ever sent over the wire. It's a hash on the client side and it's a hash on the domain controller, so that is used to encrypt, and then it's sent back. The client can decrypt that first part. It cannot decrypt the second part because it doesn't have that, only the service does, but the client will encrypt that second piece along with a timestamp, which is referred to as an authenticator, and it sends that service ticket over to the service or the server that it needs to connect to. The server can then decrypt because, again, it has that information that only it can decrypt, so that's where this mutual authentication is going back and forth. Only the client can do what it can do because it's the only one with the password. Only that server can do what it can do, because it's the only one with the password. If anyone were to capture that in between, it's not going to do much good, because, again, we have things timestamped as well, so that prevents replay attacks. Once all this is done and the service looks up and says, I trust the KDC, the client trusts the KDC, the KDC says, yes, the client is valid, go ahead and grant that service, they connect. Going forward, each time that needs to happen again, rather than having to go through this process for every single connection, you get what's called a ticket-granting ticket. That takes that first part out of the loop, so the next time it needs to make a connection, the client goes to the KDC, to the authentication service, requests that TGT, send that over to the service, and that's encrypted by the session key that was originally set up with that AS. It only has an 8-hour lifespan, Every so often that's going to need to be regenerated. But the point of that is, the very first time it needs to connect to a service it's going to go through the process, encrypt, get those two pieces sent to it, it's going to be able to decrypt one. It'll re-encrypt the second piece along with the timestamp, send it over to the service, the service can decrypt. Next time around, it uses a ticket-granting ticket to shortcut that process so it doesn't have to re-authenticate. It's already valid with a session key that's valid, again, for 8-10 hours, so that way it can just pass directly over to the service and make a connection.

Attribute Based Access Control (ABAC)
Attribute-based access control, or ABAC, it's dynamic, so it's considered more or less the

"next-gen" authorization mechanism, and its policies comprised of attributes that can be about anything or anyone. We can get very granular, and it's not confined to a set of predefined rules or a specific type of role. It allows for set-valued and also atomic-valued granularity, and that can be combined for complex Boolean rule sets. Let's take a look at what comprises attribute-based access control. We have three things at the architecture level. We have a Policy Enforcement Point, or a PEP, and that protects the resources being accessed. The PEP generates authorization requests and sends it to what's referred to as the PDP, so that is the Policy Decision Point. The PDP evaluates incoming requests against configuration policies. The PDP permits or denies and may request additional information, metadata in other words, from something referred to as a Policy Information Point, or a PIP. The PIP is a bridge between the PDP, the Policy Decision Point, and external sources of information such as LDAP, specific databases. You can get very granular as to say who can do what. If a person is a specific type of role, perhaps, if they have a certain type of clearance, perhaps, if they're trying to do a specific type of action. If we look at that in more detail, these specific attributes, we have subject attributes, so that could be anything about the user requesting access. It could be their age, security clearance or their job title. All of these are specific things that you can use to key off of when granting or denying access to a specific resource. Next, we have action attributes. That refers to the action, or actions, being attempted, whether it's read, write, delete, approve, deny. And then we have resource and object attributes, and that describes the object being accessed, the type, the department, the classification, the sensitivity. Much more granular when we start combining all of these things together, who they are, where they're coming from, their age, their clearance, their title, combined with who the user is, what action they're trying to do, what object they're trying to access. Then we have contextual or environment attributes, and this can be things like time, location, or other dynamic aspects. When you combine all of these things together, as you can imagine, you can get a very complex if/then Boolean type of logic around decision making. What it does is it gives us that granular, dynamic ability to provision. We don't have to do things ahead of time. We can let it happened on the fly, depending upon who that user is, where they are, what their title is. As they move throughout the day, move throughout locations, as they change titles, that specific, read, write, delete, approve, deny, all of those things will change, as the attribute about that person changes.

Rule-based/Role-based Access Control (RBAC)

Next, we have rule-based access control, and RBAC is used in two separate context. In this specific one, we're talking of a predefined or a preconfigured security policy and that's going to define and decide access. We could say explicitly deny all of those, except in an allow list, or we could say deny only those who specifically appear in a denial list. It's very much a list-based control mechanism, it's more flexible than MAC or mandatory access control, but less flexible than discretionary access control. That list is configured ahead of time. Then we have another role-based access control, or RBAC, context and that is a role-based access control and that access is based, on the user's role. Group membership determines what a user can and can't do, so that's pretty much how most enterprise operating systems and most enterprise environments are functioning. So once a user changes roles, then their access will change accordingly. As an example, a user might be moving from human resources to finance. So if we have a few folks that are in human resources. If they move over to finance, well they're going to lose access to that human resource document and all those files and folders. However, they're going to gain access to the payroll files. Just by virtue of moving from one group to another, they're going to lose access to their old stuff, but they're going to gain access to their new stuff. It's easy to manage, an administrator doesn't have to go in and specifically give s to each individual person, he can pre-configure those rules and those access s to a group, that way, when people come in and out of that group, they're automatically granted those permissions.

Access Control Methods

There are four main methods of access control that I want you to be aware of for the exam. We have mandatory access control. Or MACs, and that is very inflexible and it's very rigid, but it's also the most secure. Things are written in stone, there is no flexibility, no one can pass your information on to somebody else, it's very, very inflexible. Next, we have discretionary access control lists, and they are a little more dynamic, they're flexible, they're also the least secure so things can change on the fly. Then we have role-based access control, or RBAC. Role-based access control is access based on a role or a group membership. This is what pertains typically in a Kerberos environment, Linux environment, Apple, and also within Microsoft's Active Directory. You place users into groups, you give access to those groups. If you pull a user out of a group, then that access gives away. Then last we have rule-based access control, again, using RBAC, so that's access based on a predefined list. That is saying, if you're on the list you're in, if you're not, you're not. We can either have explicit permit or explicit deny lists depending upon how we have things set up.

Mandatory Access Control (MAC)
Mandatory access control, or MAC, is a predefined set of capabilities and access to information, who can share what and also to whom. As an example, we have a finance folder here we can control who has access to what files and folders, but we can also control, this is written into the program, or it's controlled by a centralized security administrator that says, this person has access to these files and folders, but they cannot share those files and folders with someone else. Even if they create a file, they can't share it, it's very inflexible, and it's very rigid. But it's also the most secure model. But it must be carefully thought out and planned ahead of time because, that lack of flexibility makes it very rigid. If it's not planned properly, it can be a nightmare because people cannot do their work, so it has to be very carefully thought out before it's implemented. But once it is implemented, it's also very easy to spot breaches or deviations because everything is very clearly defined, so if there's any deviation from that, it's very easy to spot.

Discretionary Access Control (DAC)

Discretionary access control, or DAC, that allows users to dynamically share information with others. This is what most environments are comprised of. It's less secure, and it's harder to control information leakage, however, it is how things get done. If I create a file or a folder, I should be able to share that with someone else, that's the general thinking. I may not necessarily be able to share someone else's documents, but if I'm in control of my own stuff, I should be able to say this person can view it, or copy, delete, or this person cannot, I should have control over that. In a mandatory access control environment, there is no flexibility. In a discretionary access, we have that flexibility, but again, less secure, but there is the opportunity for information leakage.

Conditional Access

This is a policy-based access framework based upon if/then type logic to determine the level of access or actions required. We're talking typically around cloud-based services, cloud-based applications, in this case, a software application as a service, or a SaaS application. If it's a certain user or part of a certain user group, or perhaps maybe if it's a certain type of device, or a certain network, or a certain network location, or even a certain application, well, if it's any one of those things, then we could apply policy and say, then either block access, or we could say, then require multi-factor authentication. Let's say, for instance, if a user is part of a specific group, and they're using a specific device, and they're trying to access a specific application, then require multi-factor authentication, or we could say block that, or we could say we're going to require a password change the next time they log in. All of these things can be done programmatically from the portal or from the configuration tool set, but the takeaway being conditional access is based around an if/then type of methodology. If a user or a device meets these certain set of criteria, and then apply some type of action.

Privileged Accounts

Privileged accounts should only be used sparingly as well. We should use non-admin accounts, non-privileged accounts, for most normal day to day activities. Non-admin accounts reduce the likelihood that something can get installed in our systems and in our environment that we don't want, and if they do happen to get installed, it does with a reduced set of privileges. We should only have these privileged accounts to perform admin-level functions, even admins should have a non-admin account and then an admin account. They would use their lower level account when they want to do day to day activities, and then when they want to do something that is administrative, they would execute that account under that admin account, whether it's an administrator account or pseudo account, it depends upon the operating system, but use those things sparingly. Users, should use non-admin accounts for their daily tasks and their daily activities. Invoke privileged accounts when necessary to perform specific tasks. Separation of those accounts makes things much less likely to be abused.

Filesystem Permissions
When it comes to filesystem permissions improper permission settings on files, folders or even symbolic links, can give attackers unintended access. That means web servers, the files and folders that sit on the web server if they're accessible and they're not properly secured, it could have unintended consequences. We're also talking about database servers, file servers, pretty much any type of file system within our network, if they're not secured properly, it can have unintended consequences and it could be giving away critical information. So, Windows servers typically have read, write, and execute as their permissions. Linux servers can get more granular. But just understand that auditing should be enabled on critical, or restricted files and folders to make sure that these things are secured properly, and also that they stay

that way. Because it's possible, for things over time to get changed or shifted either intentionally or unintentionally, and then if we're not aware of those changes taking effect, it could have, unintended consequences, leaking personal information or confidential information, things we don't want others to see, and certainly things we don't want attackers or bad actors to have access to. In this chapter, we covered authentication management, passwords, TPM chips, HSM chapters. We talked about authentication methods, various protocols and platforms that enable authentication across our enterprise. We also talked about access control schemes, security settings, methods.

Chapter 16 How to Implement Public Key Infrastructure

In this chapter, we'll be covering implementing public key infrastructure. We'll talk about public key infrastructure along with the types of certificates, certificate formats, and then certificate concepts. What are a certificate authority and a digital certificate? But just understand that it boils down to PKI, a public key infrastructure, and that facilitates a secure communication between sender and recipient. That communication can be sent over a secure network, something internal, perhaps within a company, or it can be used to communicate over an insecure network, i.e. the internet. By using that public key/private key combination, we can encrypt, as we talked about previously, we can encrypt bulk encryption keys or symmetrical keys we can use a combination of the asymmetrical encryption functions, public key/private key, along with symmetrical functions, which gives us the ability to bulk encrypt, stream large amounts of data quickly, and the combination of the two allow us to securely communicate over that insecure medium.

Certificate Authority
A certificate authority can be internal to our organization or it can be external. As an example,

we have one that's external, it's going to live out on the internet, and it will be used as a trusted third party for both Bob and the financial institution, in this case, a bank. They want to communicate. Bob wants to initiate some transaction. So, the certificate authorities that are out on the internet can be Thawte, they can be Verisign. There are a number of major certificate authorities that provide credentials pretty much for the majority of the internet and most of the companies on the internet. The CA is trusted by both Bob and the bank. When Bob connects to the bank the first time, he's presented with that bank's public key if he wants to establish a secure communication channel. He has the public key that's given to him by the bank. He will use that public key to encrypt session keys that he sends back to the bank. The financial institution is the only one that can decrypt that communication because they have the private key. Bob can be sure that the bank is the only one that can decrypt. Bob can also, if need be, verify the credentials that were presented to him with that certificate authority and make sure that they're still valid. Just like if a police officer pulls you over and checks your credentials, check your license, he's going to trust the state to issue a valid set of credentials. He can check the CRL. He can either go into his mobile terminal or call dispatch and say, let me run this driver's license and see if it comes back as valid. If it does, then he can proceed either giving a warning or a ticket or, whatever he's going to do, but he checks the validity of that credential. Bob can check against the CRL to make sure that it is in fact valid. Assuming that it is, he will encrypt the session key he's used to communicate; he'll send that back. The bank is the only one that can decrypt. It will decrypt that communication, extract session keys, and they have a bulk encryption algorithm they can use to establish further communication over that TLS or SSL channel. It's encrypted, and it's secure.

CRLs

A CRL, or a client revocation list is published by the certificate authorities, and it's used to inform clients that certificates have been revoked or are no longer valid. Where a police officer pulls someone over and checks their license, they're going to check it either on their own mobile terminal, they'll run it against some type of state database, or they'll call into dispatch and say, hey, run this license for me, if that comes back as valid, well then you can go ahead and proceed. If it's been revoked, suspended, it's no longer valid and not in use. If a digital certificate is in fact on that CRL, it can exist in one of two states. We have revoked, which is irrevocable, or we have a hold or a temporary, which means it can be reversed. We have our digital certificate, if in fact it's been revoked, or irrevocable, that means it's done, it cannot be retrieved. Typically that's for a lost or compromised key, so a company can say, I think I've lost this key or I know for a fact it's been compromised, it will be revoked, pulled out of service, placed on that CRL as irrevocable, revoked. That way, no one else can use that certificate or try to initiate any fraudulent transaction. A hold is temporary, that can be reversed. With a hold, we can pull that back off again. Situations there, a client may think they lost their key or they think it may have been compromised, but then they later find out that it has not been, so they either find it or they have definitive proof that it has not been compromised. They can have that hold reversed and that digital certificate placed back into general use.

OCSP

OCSP, or an Online Certificate Status Protocol, and that's used to obtain revocation status of X.509 digital certificates. When we say X.509, we've talked about that previously, that is the format that digital certificates are issued in, it defines what information is contained within those certificates. It's an alternative to CRL, so the client revocation list. The benefits of using OCSP versus a CRL is the fact that OCSPs contain less information, so it puts less burden on the network and the client resources. If you have a very large environment, then you're constantly doing this type of communication back and forth, checking these certificates, using OCSP will contain less information, still gives you what you need, you can tell if a certificate is valid or not, but it contains less information and will put less of a burden, network traffic, in other words, on that network. As an example, so Bob and Alice, they want to exchange communication. Alice wants to communicate with Bob, or Bob with Alice, vice versa. Well, when that happens, Alice will send her public key to Bob, he'll use that key to then exchange communication, he'll create the session key, send that off to Alice, she can decrypt, and then they can communicate over TLS or SSL. Well, what Bob can do in the meantime, however, is once he gets that public key from Alice, he can send an OCSP request to an OCSP responder, that's the terminology used for what these devices are. So that OCSP request goes out, the OCSP responder will check their database to see if that certificate is in fact on there. If it is, they'll respond back and say, hey, you may not want to talk to Alice, she's been compromised, or they'll respond back and say, nope, you're good to go, go ahead establish communication, at which point Bob uses Alice's public key, encrypts session keys and sends it off, and the same process happens as before, communication is then established over SSL and

TLS, and they have a secure communication channel from thereafter.

CSR and PKCS Standards

Next we have is a CSR, or certificate signing request, and in this case, an applicant will apply to a certificate authority, or a CA, for a digital certificate. PKCS #10 is the most common type, and PKCS stands for public key cryptography standards, and here is the information that's contained in that request. We have a common name, the business name, department, city, state, and country, and then the email address. So some basic information about that entity that is, in fact, requesting that digital certificate. Just for your own information, the PKCS standards go through 1 through 15. The ones we've more or less focused on throughout this book would be number five, password-based encryption standards, and also PKCS #10, which is what we just talked about the certification request standard.

PKI

PKI stands for public key infrastructure, and it is the components that enable the usage of digital certificates, and that public key/private key cryptography or encryption, and that's going to include hardware, software, people, policies, and also procedures. Before we get too further along, I want to make sure you understand that when you visit a website, as we've talked about in our previous example, let's say that Bob wants to visit that financial institution. You might ask, well, where do these digital certificates come from? Well, they're built into our web browsers. In Firefox, if we go to Advanced Options, then go down to Options. Each web browser is slightly different, but they all contain roughly the same options. Under the Certificates section, it says requests, When a server requests my personal certificate, I can select one automatically or ask me every time. And then you see Query the OCSP responder. When Bob visits that bank, it's going to query the OCSP responder and say, hey, is this certificate that I'm being presented with, is this public key valid, is that certificate still valid, can I process it? And then we click on View Certificates, and this is all the certificate authorities, they have some pre-made or pre-canned certificates that are issued throughout all of our browsers. That allows us to have a built-in trust up to the root certificates, and there's a number of them. We see the SHA-256 Fingerprint or the SHA1 Fingerprint, we know where it's issued from, the Common Name, the Organization, when it Begins, when it Expires. We can click on the Details, and then look at the Serial Number, or the Certificate, the Certification Algorithm, it's a SHA1 with an RSA Encryption. We can look at things like the Public Key, so this is the actual public key that's presented to someone that wants to communicate, and if they want to encrypt something, they can use this public key to then encrypt, which the recipient has the private key to decrypt. Getting back into the details of PKI, there are a number of components that make up a PKI environment, that public key infrastructure. The public key infrastructure is comprised of the certificate authority, or the CA. That issues and verifies digital certificates. Next, we have a registration authority, or an RA. That's going to verify the identity of users requesting information from the CA. Sometimes they're referred to as subordinate CAs. We also have a central directory, so that's a secure location in which to store and index keys, so that's going to be typically on an internal network. Then we have a certificate management system, so a method to manage valid certificates, publish CRLs. Then we have certificate policy, which defines who can request, issue, and use certificates, and of course what purpose can those certificates be used for? As you're studying for the exam, it's important that you understand what each of these components are and how they fit into the PKI environment.

Public Key

Public key is something that we should be familiar with at this point, but a public key is one part of a PKI, or a public key infrastructure, used to encrypt or to decrypt data. Remember, a public key can encrypt or decrypt just like a private key can encrypt or decrypt. It's a mathematically linked key pair that has a corresponding private key. The public key is designed, as the name implies, to be made publicly available to anyone. If I want someone to be able to communicate with me in a secure fashion, I can give them my public key. They can then encrypt communication, a document, an email file, to me that only I can decrypt. Also, they can use that public key to encrypt session keys, so they can instantiate that communication, that TLS/SSL communication going forward. They'll send me those bulk encryption session keys, those symmetric keys. I can use my private key to decrypt, extract those session keys, and then communicate. Just to reiterate, the private key must be kept secret. If that gets compromised, then all bets are off, anything that you have that's been encrypted can be decrypted with that private key. It's very important that that be kept private.

Private Key

A private key is one part of that public key infrastructure, PKI, used to encrypt or decrypt. That's something to keep in mind that I want to say a few times just to make sure it sinks in. A public key can encrypt or decrypt, and a private key can encrypt or decrypt. However, they cannot do the same on an existing piece of data. If you encrypt with the public key, you'll decrypt with the private, or if you encrypt with the private, you'll decrypt with the public. It's a mathematically linked key pair that has a corresponding public key, in this instance, and the private key is, as the name implies, designed to be kept private. That should not be given to anyone.

Object Identifiers (OID)

Object identifiers, or OIDs are incorporated into a PKI, or a public key infrastructure and they're used to assign one or more certificate policies to a given CA, or certificate authority. OIDs are built-in to Active Directory Certificate Services, or ADCS, as an example, can be randomly assigned for internal use only, can also be public or private. An organization can register a public OID to enable that organization's PKI to work with another organization's PKI, so if there is some interoperability that needs to happen there, you can register it publicly so that the OIDs and so that the individual components of that PKI, the certificate policies, can transfer or work between different organizations. If we look at this in a little more detail, an organization can register a public OID, it's a two-step process. One, you would register what's called a Private Enterprise Number, or a PEN. This PEN can be applied for at the address, pen.iana.org, and the following web address, and then once complete, a unique number will be assigned or issued that will be listed at this following web page, iana.org/assignments/enterprise-numbers. And within that there is a numerical prefix that is fixed, that's not changeable, that's 1.3.6.1.4.1, if you're familiar with SNMP and MIBS, it's similar. And then from there you would append whatever your organization's name, that PEN, that Private Enterprise Number, let's say in this example it's 56789, then your OID up to this point would be 1.3.6.1.4.1.56789, and then you would append an additional number or numerical addresses after that for each subcomponent. As it drills down through the organization, you would identify additional numbers, and there are things that you would create or sign internally for your use.

Types of Certificates

Let's go ahead and talk about the various types of certificates. There's a few that I want to cover. We have wildcards, SAN, code signing, self-signed, machine or computer, email, user, root, domain validation, and extended validation. Each of these we'll cover in more detail. I just want to give you an idea of what they mean and the use cases or where they would be used in your environment. A wildcard is a digital certificate or a public key certificate that is used with multiple sub-domains of a domain. As an example, we may have *.Google.com as our main domain, that's the company domain, but we may have sub-domains within that. Well, rather than have individual SSL certificates for each of these, we can have a wildcard certificate that would allow us to secure all of the sub-domains with that same wildcard certificate. So, in other words, sales.Google.com or support.Google.com, they could all be secured with the same certificate. Next we have SAN, that's a Subject Alternate Name, not SAN as in a storage area network, but within a digital certificate or PKI infrastructure definitions it's Subject Alternate Name, and it's a certificate that allows multiple hostnames to be protected by a single certificate. Not sub-domains like a wild card, this is completely different names, completely different company names, up to 2000, in fact. If you're on a shared infrastructure and you have different hosts and different domain names, that single SAN, or Subject Alternate Name certificate can be used to secure all of those things. Next we have code signing. This is a type of digital certificate that's issued typically by a trusted CA, or certificate authority, and it's used to secure things like downloading code, macros, and objects. Many browsers won't allow code to run unless it is signed by a certificate from a trusted root, Verisign, Thawte, there are a number of them out there that are prebuilt into the browser, but they won't allow that code to run unless it's digitally signed by someone that it trusts. Next we have self signed. This is typically done to provide SSL functionality, or Secure Sockets Layer functionality in a temporary or a test and dev environment for servers that we're going to be temporarily using or in a very low secure environment. It would not be used for something in production, something public facing, but if we need that SSL functionality for testing, this works great. Or if it's in a very low, secure environment, that's internal use only, again, not an issue, just not for public use. And then we have machine or computer certificates. This is used to authenticate, a machine or a computer into an Active Directory environment, as an example. Just like we can verify a sender of a specific document in email, we can also verify, and depending upon how that PKI is used, the domain can verify the machine and also the machine can verify the domain to make sure that both are in fact valid and authenticated properly. Next, email, and that's a digital certificate used, to secure and authenticate email, Used for security, but also for authentication. Then we have a user, and a user certificate is very similar to a machine certificate, but it's used to authenticate users, not machines, but it's used to authenticate that user into that AD environment. In a very secure, or a PKI infrastructure, we're going to not only validate ourselves and we're going to log in with our own credentials, we're going to have our own certificates, we're going to authenticate to the network, but our machine is also going to authenticate to the network. We have two things that are authenticating before we can access resources on that network. And then a user certificate is similar in concept to a machine certificate. It's used to authenticate a user. Just like we talked about with a machine certificate, it's used to authenticate a user in this case into an AD environment. Next we have root, and a root certificate, it's a self-signed public key certificate, we're talking about PKI here, public key infrastructure, so that certificate identifies it as a root CA, or certificate authority. Typically that's going to be an offline root that will generate certificates that are then put via USB or some removable media into our subordinate or our intermediary CAs. Domain validation is a server security certificate that provides the lowest level of validation available from a commercial enterprise. We can get them pretty cheap out on the Internet, and what happens is the company that's issuing that domain validation certificate will either automate it, or in some fashion contact the point of contact for that domain. When you register you put down this person is responsible for this domain, they'll verify that, quote unquote, wink-wink, and then issue that certificate. It's not very secure and is subject to spam and other types of misuse. Domain validation is a legitimate commercial certificate, but it offers the lowest level of security. Next, we have extended validation, and here it's increased security over domain validation certificates due to enhanced validation process. It's very similar as far as what you need to do to register for one, but the actual validation process is enhanced, "high assurance", meaning they have a human call in, validate that these people are who they say they are. Can it be misused? Of course, we can put in information that is bogus, and someone could validate that bogus information, so it doesn't 100% guarantee anything, but it does provide enhanced security over a simple domain validation.

Certificate Formats
A few certificate formats that we should be aware of. We have PEM, or P-E-M. This is the most common format that CAs issue, and they can have several extensions, .pem,.crt,.cer, and .key extensions. It's Base64 encoded, and it's an ASCII file. Next, we have DER, certificates. This is a binary form of the certificate instead of the ASCII PEM format. It can have extensions of either.der or.cer, and it's very similar to PEM certificates except it's in binary instead of in ASCII. And then we have PFX. PFX certificates, typically encrypted, and it also

typically will require a password to open. It can contain almost anything, certificates, certificate chains, or private keys, and it will have the extension of.pfx or p12,.p12. Next, we have something referred to as P7B. P7B certificates only contain certificates or certificate chains, No private keys. Also, Base64 encoded. P7Bs have the extension of.p7b, but it's also known as PKCS#7.

Online vs. Offline Certificate Authority (CA)
We need to make sure that we understand the difference between an online versus an offline certificate authority. An online certificate authority has a couple things. It's typically a subordinate CA, it's not going to be the root. It's going to be typically a subordinate CA, or certificate authority. It can, however, issue certificates. That's typically what it does. It issues certificates either to additional subordinates or further downstream subordinates, or to the actual users or the hosts that will ingest that certificate. Then, it also trusts the enterprise root CA, the enterprise root certificate authority. And then also enterprise CAs need to be joined to an Active Directory Directory Services, or an AD domain. Conversely, offline certificate root authorities, they're a trusted root CA. They're the tip of the iceberg. They are the top of the CA or the PKI hierarchy. And it's often referred to as a

standalone root. so that's installed in offline mode. We don't attach the actual root CA to the network. We do that so that it can never be compromised. It's not connected to the network, and it is also not a member of that AD domain, the AD Directory Services domain. We install it in offline mode, we're going to generate that certificate, typically it's going to be put onto a USB drive or a CD or DVD, some removable medium, we'll take that from that standalone root, and then we'll go over and sneakernet it to our subordinate CA. From there, we'll use that certificate to then issue certificates to either other subordinate CAs, or to hosts, or to things within the organization that apply or need that certificate. That way, if it's ever compromised, we can simply take that subordinate CA offline, get rid of it, and anything with it that's been issued from that subordinate CA is compromised, but the entire PKI infrastructure is not compromised. Conversely, if we had a compromise or a breach and the actual root of the entire PKI infrastructure has been compromised, then our entire PKI infrastructure, our entire security throughout the enterprise would be compromised. We purposely don't do that to avoid just that situation.

Stapling and Pinning
Another term I want you to be familiar with is something referred to as stapling. Stapling is also

known as OCSP Stapling. It's formally known as TLS Certificate Status Request extension, and we've talked about TLS before and certificates in general before as well. What happens is the certificate bearer appends or staples timestamped OCSP responses to that initial TLS handshake. That gives an added layer of security, and it also removes the need for the client to contact the certificate authority, so it helps speed up the process. Next we have pinning. Pinning is the process of associating a host with their expected x.509 certificate, which is in effect, the public key, that digital certificate. So, more than one certificate or public key for a given host can be possible, and if so, then it's added to what's called a pin set. What we're doing is speeding up the process a bit, and we're also refining or narrowing what we expect that host to have.

Trust Models

When it comes to trust models, a couple things to be aware of. The first model is referred to as a hierarchical trust model, that's a single root CA that digitally signs all certificates. That's for small environments. We don't have a very distributed or a very large PKI infrastructure so that root, that single root CA could in fact sign all of the certificates, not recommended not in use in larger environments, but for smaller environments, you need to know that it exists. And the next model is referred to as a distributed trust model. In this model, we have multiple CAs with one master root CA, That route CA is installed on offline mode and what that does is it limits the risk if one of the CAs is, in fact, compromised before, and then it also distributes the load throughout the infrastructure. As an example, we have our root CA, that's going to be installed on offline mode, and will issue digital certificates, we're going to take that via USB or some removable media, so we'll take that from the offline root, and then use that to configure our intermediary CAs. Those intermediary CAs are the ones that will issue the certificates to clients. One other trust model I want you to be aware of is something referred to as the Web of Trust, or the WoT. That's going to be used in smaller environments or end user communication with no centralized certificate authority. So for the most part, if you're in a small to medium-sized business or anything larger or an enterprise, you're going to have some type of formalized PKI infrastructure, but in instances where there is no centralized CA and a Web of Trust can, in fact, be used. Commonly used with such things as PGP, which is pretty good privacy, is the public key private key encryption mechanism we use to encrypt files or emails, so it's commonly used when communication between two parties, they wish to communicate using what's called self-generated or self-signed encryption keys.

Key Escrow

A key escrow is a trusted third-party that's going to hold the keys needed to decrypt data, so to use in cases where keys are lost or some mandate, i. e. a court order or some situation that requires the decryption of data, it's also referred to as a fair crypto system., as you can imagine, there are some disagreements around the technical feasibility of having a trusted, third-party that can correctly manage access to keys or control collateral compromise if those keys are leaked. We all know that that never happens, I understand, but theoretically, if it did happen, how can we control that if a third-party manages all of our keys or perhaps they manage the keys for a number of different organizations, well, in doing so, we create some risk. There is definitely some historical precedent, it happens more often, cases where organizations are being breached, at record scale, hackers are becoming more and more sophisticated. The idea of having some trusted third-party hold all of our encryption keys, I'm not so sure uncomfortable with that. That's a business decision that you may have, there may be cases where you have to have that again, perhaps a court order or something where it needs to be kept so that law enforcement or whoever can get access to those keys if need be, but That's a case by case basis and something that you, as the security professional within your own organization would need to decide, work with your business units to come up with the best solution.

Certificate Chaining

With certificate chaining, we have something referred to as the path of trust, and that path of trust goes from a user certificate extends all the way up to the root certificate. As an example we have the root CA all the way down to the end certificate. That path of trust extends from that end certificate all the way up to the root CA, or the root certificate authority, and that allows us to ensure that everything is secure from the root down. Conversely, if the root is compromised, everything below that is potentially compromised, we can't trust anything that is valid and has not been tampered with. We made it to the end of the book. In this chapter, we talked about four main areas, we talked about PKI components, we talked about types of certificates, and then we covered certificate formats, and then lastly, concepts around certificates.

Conclusion

Congratulations on completing this book! I am sure you have plenty on your belt, but please don't forget to leave an honest review. Furthermore, if you think this information was helpful to you, please share anyone who you think would be interested of IT as well.

About Richie Miller

Richie Miller has always loved teaching people Technology. He graduated with a degree in radio production with a minor in theatre in order to be a better communicator. While teaching at the Miami Radio and Television Broadcasting Academy, Richie was able to do voiceover work at a technical training company specializing in live online classes in Microsoft, Cisco, and CompTia technologies. Over the years, he became one of the top virtual instructors at several training companies, while also speaking at many tech and training conferences. Richie specializes in Project Management and ITIL these days, while also doing his best to be a good husband and father.

www.ingramcontent.com/pod-product-compliance
Lightning Source LLC
Chambersburg PA
CBHW071233050326
40690CB00011B/2093